D1566684

Narsingh Deo

TRAVELS
IN
COMPUTERLAND

PRESENTED
TO THE
UCF LIBRARY
BY

DR. N. DEO

TRAVELS
IN
COMPUTERLAND;

OR,
INCOMPATIBILITIES and INTERFACES
A *Full and True* Account of the IMPLEMENTATION
of the *LONDON STAGE* INFORMATION BANK

---

by a Professor of *English*
BEN ROSS SCHNEIDER, Jr.
M.A., P.H.D., F.R.S.A.

Written by
HIMSELF

My ill Fate pushed me on now with an Obstinacy that nothing could resist; and though I had several times loud Calls from my Reason and my more composed Judgment to go Home, yet I had no Power to do it.

ROBINSON CRUSOE.

I could not reject his Proposal, the Thirst I had of seeing the World, notwithstanding my past Misfortunes, continuing as violent as ever.　　　LEMUEL GULLIVER.

How dull it is to pause, to make an end.

ULYSSES.

♦♦ Printed for
ADDISON-WESLEY PUBLISHING COMPANY
Reading, Massachusetts　•　Menlo Park, California
London　•　Amsterdam　•　Don Mills, Ontario　•　Sydney

Copyright © 1974 by Addison-Wesley Publishing Company, Inc. Philippines copyright 1974 by Addison-Wesley Publishing Company, Inc.

All rights reserved. No part of this publication may be reproduced, stored in a retrieval system, or transmitted, in any form or by any means, electronic, mechanical, photocopying, recording, or otherwise, without the prior written permission of the publisher. Printed in the United States of America. Published simultaneously in Canada. Library of Congress Catalog Card No. 74-9250.

ISBN 0-201-06737-4
ABCDEFGHIJ-AL-7987654

TABLE OF
CONTENTS

For Dear Boo

CHAPTER I

A PARAMETRIC

The Author's apology to the Reader. His definition of a Computer.

Three summers ago, the wife of a doctor, my brother-in-law's wife, to be exact, whom my family and I were visiting at her and his idyllic spot on Lake Michigan, after watching me, an English teacher, fuss, fume, gnash teeth, and eat gelusil for several days over things like throughput, turnaround, and quality control, on long distance to Kansas City, New York, and Appleton, Wisconsin—all of which were distracting me terribly from the full enjoyment of the idyllic spot—this worthy, wise, and perfectly gorgeous mother of three and grandmother of one, gracious hostess of myriads of always grateful guests, asked me in impassioned tones suggestive of an emotion long pent up, "How in Heaven's name can an English professor with your long experience and talent devote his entire energy to the piddling details of a computer project about obsolete theatrical affairs when our youth need more than ever before the guidance and knowledge of good teachers in the classroom?" Granting the dubious premise that my rapidly souring presence in the classroom has value for a generation gifted with total vision at birth, and I suppose that any veteran teacher should at least consider the possibility, that

1

question, seeming to come from the depths of her being, reached me at the core of mine.

I realized that when the chance had come to stop racking my brains for ways of getting a response to *The Prelude* and *A Tale of a Tub* and grading all the papers I thought I should assign, in order to become the director of a computer project I had dreamed of and for several years promoted, I had welcomed it as the sound of water in a weary land: it was a clean break with a monotonous past; a ray of recognition in a dim life; a chance to show what I could do and silence doubters; a victory of humanists over scientists, among many defeats, in the battle for funds; a voyage of discovery to an unknown territory of knowledge. In the year of the totally new life that followed my initial acceptance of the undertaking, no doubts about its value had entered my mind until she voiced them. Then it came home to me crushingly that, in the excitement of really doing things instead of just thinking about them, I had led a shamelessly unexamined life, that I was no better than one of the thoughtless herd.

My sister-in-law expressed for me, in classic purity, the layman's longstanding doubts about the existence of literary research and doubts of shorter duration, shared indeed by most of the literary profession itself, about the possibility of finding out anything useful concerning a work of art by means of a machine. Everyone accepts the fact that scientific research, however abstruse, eventually contributes to human welfare, but even public awareness that literary research goes on is low. That it could in any way benefit mankind is not recognized at all, even by many of its practitioners. It bewilders many, therefore, if it be granted that a literary scholar does any research at all, that he should do it by computer. Literary scholars do, of course, like chemists and psychologists, conduct research and publish the results of their research for the general advance of knowledge of the subject. Their works, though numerous, are rarely read by laymen. They have scores of special journals and write hundreds of books yearly. The immediate purpose of many such works may be to clear up a fairly minute biographical, historical, textual, or critical question. But the ultimate purpose of all works is a better understanding of literary texts, of the written word, and of language itself. I submit that this is no mean undertaking, really. After all, when considered in the largest sense, language is the foundation of that human understanding we strive so hard to promote.

It is hard to tell a doctor's wife, over martinis, that a good commentary on *Othello* may save lives, in an indirect way very devious to trace under any circumstances, but it is even more difficult to suggest how a computer analysis of the casting of *Othello* in 18th century plays may have practical value. On hearing that I proposed to put a lot of information about 18th century theatre into a computer, few laymen have been able to suppress an impolitic curiosity. "Sounds fascinating. Now what are you going to do with that when you get it all together?" Even more difficult for the world to understand might be how five scholars could spend thirty-five years compiling the eleven-volume record of performances that I wished to make accessible to the computer. In the attempt to answer such questions as these for them and for myself I endeavor to give some account of what has come to be known as the *London Stage* Information Bank project.

Part of the difficulty in accepting the computer as a tool of literary research is widespread confusion about what a computer is. For one thing, we have given it the wrong name. In French it is more accurately called an "ordinateur," or organizer. The first mistake is to assume that computers are for doing math. This notion helps to further what I think of as the computer myth, which is one branch of the mad scientist myth. The classic mad scientist is Frankenstein, who usurped God's or Nature's prerogative by attempting to create intelligent life—with what monstrous results we all know. The monster has two characteristics that carry over to the computer of our imagination. He has superhuman power, but at the same time a subhuman sensitivity that causes him to use it in ruthless, indiscriminate, mechanical, and ruthless ways. Whatever the reason, we endow the computer with the same contradictory characteristics. At one time we see it as astoundingly brilliant and at another brutally stupid. While these opposite notions prevail, the ways in which computers may help research in the humanities (or help humanity) are not likely to reveal themselves.

The brutally stupid computer is a commonplace of computer anecdotes. A lady kept getting a bill for $00.00. At first she paid no attention to it. But then the computer began to send her notes threatening worse and worse retaliation unless she paid up immediately, and finally decreeing that her credit rating in the world would be taken away forever. In desperation, after countless frantic notes of self-justification had brought no acknowledgement whatsoever, she sent the computer a check for $00.00. The bills stopped coming. If she had been able to get the ear of a human being, like as not the person would have told her, "The computer made a mistake." But the machine did not make a mistake, and the sooner the corporations who use them put the blame on the people who did, the sooner the computer will stop making mistakes. When an airplane crashes, we don't blame the airplane.

The reason for computer atrocities like this, perhaps, is management's belief in the opposite myth, that the computer is infallibly wise. This is the computer of our jokelore. A typical story goes like this: A young business executive in Chicago confronted his firm's computer with the challenge, "If you're so smart, tell me what my father is doing now." With the speed of light the computer's typewriter banged out the answer. "YOUR FATHER IS PLAY-ING GOLF AT THE IDLEWILD GOLF COURSE IN JAMAICA PLAIN, MASSACHUSETTS." "Ha, ha, got you there," said the young man. "My father is in Buffalo. I just talked to him on the telephone." "YES," typed the computer, "THAT IS YOUR MOTHER'S HUSBAND. YOUR FATHER IS PLAYING GOLF AT THE IDLEWILD GOLF COURSE IN JA-MAICA PLAIN, MASSACHUSETTS." There is some truth in the story, to be sure. The young man is indeed some sort of an abomination for entrusting the computer with such delicate questions as paternity. The joke within the joke is that he gets his just deserts from this Godlike machine. But we think this same deity too stupid to give credit where credit is due.

A computer, to me, is a machine that reads. Reading implies comprehension, and in a limited sense, computers comprehend. I imagine that the computer recognizes a word in a text by some process as this: Supposing it is to recognize the word "man" in the sentence "The dog bit the man;" it attempts to match the word "man" to each word in the sentence, beginning at the beginning. The matching attempt could not take place unless the machine were capable of doing the desired thing when it fails. This is where the program comes in. "If no match, try next word," says the program. Thus the computer "loops" along, trying "The," "dog," "bit," "the," until it at last lands on "man." "If match, print sentence," says the program. Or "If match, ring a bell," or "If match, call police," or "If match, remember the sentence," or "If match, add one to the 'man' count," or "If match, look for 'dog' in sentence and if 'dog,' print sentence," or "If match, turn off." The possibilities of this "if, then" way of proceeding are endless. And this is how, although I have heard of no computers that know what a dog looks or smells like or how fast its tail wags, they comprehend in a limited sense what they read.

If the following account serves to show the dangers that beset those who compute while pointing the way to beneficial uses, it will serve its purpose. My thesis is that the key to both its inadequacies and its virtues is the recognition of its essential simplicity. My tale is indeed all too true, being compiled entirely from accumulated letters, notes, and documents. Conversations are approximate, of course, and I have occasionally stretched a point for truth of impression. But I have records to support even the most incredible tales that I shall unfold.

CHAPTER II

OF FEASIBILITY

The author becomes entangled in the London Stage Information Bank & conceives of a Pilot Project. He questions Administrators & Computer Scientists, visits Widener Library & the Association for Computing Machinery, where he encounters a Living Advertisement. He considers the scarcity of Funds,. and draws to an Inside Straight.

A lthough I had dabbled in computing before, my first invitation to embark on a fully equipped expedition to this never-never land of promises and frustrations did not come until the 15th of April in 1970, when I received a letter from Professor George Winchester Stone, Jr., Dean of the Graduate School of New York University, whom I knew as having been the executive secretary of the Modern Language Association of America and as an editor of *The London Stage, 1660–1800, A Calendar of Plays, Entertainment & Afterpieces, Together with Casts, Box-receipts and Contemporary Comment, Compiled from the Playbills, Newspapers & Theatrical Diaries of the Period,* edited with critical introductions by William van Lennep, Emmett L. Avery, Arthur H. Scouten, George Winchester Stone, Jr. & Charles Beecher Hogan. Carbondale, Illinois:

Southern Illinois University Press, 1960–1968, eleven volumes, 8026 pages. Dean Stone wrote: "Your evident interest in and knowledge of computers and their application to the field of humanities, as well as your long interest in the field covered by *The London Stage*, prompts me to ask you if you are interested in joining this project by directing a computerized index of this eleven-volume work."

His evidence of my interest had been an article published three years earlier in *Theatre Notebook* with the eye-catching title of "The Coquette-Prude as an Actress's Line in Restoration Comedy during the Time of Mrs. Oldfield." Here I had attempted to prove by computer analysis of cast lists in *The London Stage* that such a thing as a "coquette-prude" actually walked the boards nightly in the early 18th century. If I could prove this, it would help me to establish that playwrights almost always worked this character into their plays. If I could prove this, it would help me to establish that certain characters in well-known comedies of the period were in fact "coquette-prudes." If I could prove this, it would make my argument more convincing that these plays had a serious purpose. And if that were true as well, it followed as the night the day that most 20th century critics, who presented them as light entertainment, totally missed their point, causing the directors of their frequent revivals on the stage to so badly misdirect them that they had precisely the opposite effect on audiences from what they were supposed to have.

It was to pound home this one nail in my jackbuilt house that I first consulted *The London Stage, 1660–1800*, back in 1964. From analysis of plays I amassed a list of 1027 characters, each of whom I tagged with several of a possible 113 characteristics like young, old, good, bad, married, single, chaste, unchaste, gay, grave, coquette, booby, hoyden, fop, and so forth. The problem was to find out whether any of these characteristics clustered in the roles of any actors and actresses to the extent that I could determine their "lines" or specialties, their favorite stock characters. During the ninety-year period when these 1027 characters were most prominent on the stage, some 200 actors flourished, performing the 1027 characters close to 30,000 times, according to *The London Stage*. 113 characteristics × 1027 roles × 30,000 performances, according to my arithmetic, equals 318 million, 500 thousand instances of a characteristic appearing on the stage.

The London Stage contained simply too much of the kind of evidence I wanted. But I could not ignore any single bit of it for fear that it might be crucial. Further, the evidence was presented in an inconvenient way for the use I wished to make of it. Imagine being given a copy of the Manhattan telephone directory and being asked to find out what subscribers live on each street, and you have some idea of the task with which I was confronted. Just as the telephone book is not arranged by street, so *The London Stage* was not arranged by character. It consisted of theatre programs, arranged chronologically, day by day, year by year. As a first step, I would have to rearrange it all by role. As a second step, I would have to rearrange it all by actor. I could do it only by making out a note card for each performance of a role by an actor, giving role, actor, date, theatre, relevant performance facts, and characteristics of the role.

When I was pondering these things in my office on the fourth floor of Main Hall one bleak afternoon of March or April, 1964, my advisee and student, Charles Lord, a math major in the process of becoming an English major, stuck his head in the door to say hello, as he was wont to do on those occasions when for one reason or another he found himself at the top of the long stair climb.

In the course of passing the time of day, he expressed some disgust at the prospect of another dull summer job as a lifeguard (I think it was) and wondered whether there might not be some professor needing a research assistant.

Perhaps because he was a mathematician, the thought of doing my analysis of casting by computer flashed for the first time into my mind. "Why doesn't he keypunch all my note cards," I said to myself, "so that the computer can enter the role characteristics automatically, and then sort and tabulate the resulting cards?" But who would pay him? Just a few days earlier, I recalled, the fourth floor grapevine had carried the news that part of the Social Science Fund for Student-Faculty Research Projects was in danger of going unused. Yes, I knew of a professor who needed a research assistant, if theatre history qualified as a social study. It did. That summer Charles punched 30,000 IBM cards (fifteen boxes of them) in what I now know must have been the world's record for fast, errorless, and (I confess) cheap computer data entry. In due course the cards were sorted in several interesting ways and the outlines of the coquette-prude slowly emerged from the formerly shapeless mass.

I could not help thinking, though, during the months of keypunching and processing that ensued after Charles had stuck his head in my door, how much easier it would have been for me if *The London Stage* had already existed in a form that a computer could "read." We could then give it the list of 1027 roles, have it sort performances of them as desired, and save thereby a great deal of time and effort. If *The London Stage* had existed in a machine-readable form, I imagined that it would have taken perhaps a day at the most to compile the role-histories and actor-careers that I had needed, instead of six months. Hence at professional gatherings, I continually pestered theatre-historians with the idea that *The London Stage* ought to be put on computer tape so that the wealth of information it contained, not just about actors and roles, but about backstage affairs, box-office receipts, and contemporary comment, would be instantly accessible to all. It would be like having an index to every kind of thing in the book, from candlemakers to His Majesty the King, only the computer would even turn the pages and take notes for you. If it was worth the labor of five scholars for thirty-five years to compile and the elegant presentation given it by the Southern Illinois University Press, it was worth having in machine-readable form so that the labors I have described would not have to be repeated by every scholar who used it. The pages were so packed that an index to names, roles, and titles alone would contain about 2,000,000 entries. Not only the sheer amount of data available on many different topics pointed to computerized fact-gathering, but the very repetitive nature of these facts. The volumes already had indexes to all plays and to some names, but users of *The London Stage* who sought information on topics not covered by the index would still find so many items that computer handling would be economical. Others, like a scholar who inquired of me if a character named Mrs. Mirthwit ever occurred in plays of the early 18th century, in order to write a footnote for a new edition of Defoe's *Moll Flanders*, might have to turn over as many as a thousand pages to find out even that she was not mentioned. A highly trained scholar-teacher's time, I thought, should be better employed.

So "Yes" was the only answer I could make to Dean Stone's letter of the 13th of April (Monday, not Friday).

But could I really accomplish what I had so fervently for so long recommended? The task that I had customarily represented by a snap of the fingers now seemed monumental. I knew hardly anything about information retrieval, except that it was a vast subject. Data preparation, user interfaces, interactive query systems, search algorithms, updating techniques, and table lookups, on which I supposed millions of words had been written and dozens of conferences held, I knew only as terms vaguely connected to problems like finding coquette-prudes on the 18th century stage. I didn't know a word of FORTRAN. Nor had I any certainty that Lawrence's computer facilities, shared with and lodged in the busy and important Institute of Paper Chemistry, across the Fox River from our campus, could make room for such a large undertaking. And if it were feasible to use that facility, would Lawrence give me the time off that it probably would take? For that matter, would Lawrence see fit to harbor such a strange beast as a *London Stage* Information Bank? And where would the money come from? I imagined it might take something like twenty or thirty thousand dollars just to convert *The London Stage* to a medium that the computer could read. But even if the Institute-Lawrence computer was competent and available, and if Lawrence was willing, I had no idea how much time, money, or equipment the whole job would take. I wasn't even sure what the finished product should be.

My only recourse was to offer to conduct a "pilot project." The term sounded important and I understood it to mean that one didn't have to know what one was doing until the project was finished. This suited me fine. I would hire a programmer, I would work half-time, and together we would spend the next academic year working out the strategy for building the bank, while he wrote programs for sifting all those facts. In the end we would have the programs working on a sample of the text and a proposal for taking care of the rest.

Dean Stone approved. For several days I scurried from office to office at Lawrence, trying to get a firm hold on the local situation. I knew that some sort of ruling about science faculty devoting too much time to grants existed; perhaps the university would oppose extra-curricular humanistic empires as well. I painted as vivid a picture as I could of a Lawrence become world-famous as a center for theatre research. President Smith, a physicist, was undismayed by the thought of a computer project in the humanities. And Mr. Headrick, the new Vice President for Academic Affairs, who showed signs of wanting Lawrence to become one of the great small colleges in the land, may have looked upon a large research project as contributing in some way to this end. At any rate he favored the idea.

I determined to call next on John Bachhuber, proprietor of the computer center at the Institute of Paper Chemistry, where our work would have to be done if it were done at all. I found his den with some difficulty, for the computer is hidden somewhere under the middle of the main building of the Institute, where it lurks like a Minotaur in the middle of a labyrinth of narrow hallways, so arranged that you arrive at a boiler room or the ladies' lounge if you open the wrong door or take a wrong turn. I walked as in a French movie through an endless corridor to a doorway opening to another endless corridor, alone with the noise of my footsteps, until I reached at last two doorways. One of them was a closet. Upon opening the other I beheld an immense brightly lit glass case that appeared to contain the control room of the space ship *Enterprise*. Still I had not arrived. I found that the two doors opening into the glass case were locked, and, although I made motions to the space crew inside, they did not notice me, intent as they were on punching buttons and watching the messages appear at various stations. It was necessary to skirt the outside of the great glass cubicle, walk through a dimly lit room fitted out as a lounge but not lounged in, past a coat rack containing one raincoat, to a door that looked as if it might lead to the furnace but opened into a brightly lit anteroom full of keypunching machines. I was now at the back of the glass cubicle, in the office area.

On this April afternoon I found John Bachhuber impeccably dressed in a business suit that befitted a man in charge of over a half-million dollars worth of equipment, discussing with an assistant some mysterious codes on a large sheet of paper. John informed me that what I had heard before was true. The Institute of Paper Chemistry itself operated an information bank. It was based on abstracts of books and articles relating to paper chemistry. He showed me proudly how one could find the titles of articles on a given topic by typing key words into the computer from a terminal with a typewriter keyboard and a TV screen for a page, like the devices used by airlines to determine whether the seat you have reserved is still there. He typed "POLLUTION." The terminal almost immediately flashed the message "243 ENTRIES. LIST [them]?" John typed "NO." He then limited the items sought by typing, besides "POLLUTION," "SMOKE," and "SULPHITE." The computer reported 26 entries. He then added "WISCONSIN" and got three. Now he had the computer print the abstracts themselves. At the center of the subterranean maze a mechanical wizard was at work; as his master showed his tricks, I seemed to be listening to an incantation, containing such words as "man-machine interface," "search strategy," "Boolean statement," "conversational mode."

I asked John how they got their abstracts into the computer. Having undergone the Chinese water torture of 30,000 IBM cards six years before, I hoped that they had found a better way than the keypunch. They had indeed. And John proceeded to open the door to another marvel, called the MT/ST. MT/ST means Magnetic Tape Selectric Typewriter. It is an IBM bouncing ball typewriter that makes a magnetic tape of what it types. By a simple process, MT/ST tapes can be converted to computer tapes.

The Institute's abstract service proved that a job the size of *The London Stage* could be accomplished on the Institute's computer. They had three tape decks and three disk drives. One disk might hold the whole eleven volumes of *The London Stage*. The machine wasn't so busy that if we worked nights and weekends, we could get plenty of computer time. Now came the big question, Would we have to pay? John thought we might have to, because we were an "outside" project, not an "inside" faculty research project. I maintained that this *London Stage* research seemed no more outside than that of anyone else on either his or our faculty that had a grant to further the advance of knowledge. There the matter rested pending high-level rulings.

To get some more bearings to pilot by, I next decided to consult Lewis Sawin, Associate Dean of Arts and Sciences at the University of Colorado, one of the few literary scholars I knew who had engineered an information bank. He was coeditor, with Sally Sedelow, of a new journal called *Computer Studies in the Humanities and Verbal Behavior*. I had first become acquainted with his Automated Bibliography of American Literature five years earlier at a conference on Humanistic Applications of Computers sponsored by IBM at Purdue, one of a series they had scattered strategically all over the United States during the middle and late sixties to acquaint non-computing humanists with computing humanists.

The star of this conference, as far as I was concerned,

was Sally Sedelow, a Smith and Bryn Mawr girl with a Ph.D. in medieval English literature, who had been working on an immense Navy contract with the Rand Corporation to develop a system for analyzing the thematic content of Shakespeare's *Hamlet* and Russian scientific documents. Despite this unlikely connection with the military, she struck me as a sane and good-humored advocate of literary analysis by computer. Two of the things she said were prophetic: that the humanists have an ingrained opposition to computing based on ignorance of how and where the machine can help them; and that university computer centers, accustomed to neat scientific calculations on small amounts of data, were usually swamped when messy humanistic projects came along with great piles of text to be processed over and over again. With 8026 pages of data, I felt I would test the truth of that principle if my hopes were realized.

At this same conference, a computing genius named Curt Benster, having no institutional or corporational address, and Donald Kraft, IBM Industry Representative for Information Retrieval, made indelible impressions on me. As I remember it, Benster burst in passionately on Kraft at a sort of free-for-all windup session. Kraft had based his talk on what he said was going to be IBM's new policy: no more punchcards; no more incomprehensible codes; no more arbitrary abbreviations; no more abstract symbols. Instead, IBM's new motto was "English in and English out." Benster rose to his feet shouting agreement. "Natural language! No keypunching! No keystroking of any kind! FOLLOW COPY! Today we have optical scanning. Soon we will have vocal input!" I could see him a century earlier careening down a Colorado canyon on Jimmy Stewart legs shouting, "Gold!" When the meeting broke up I gravitated toward Benster. I started to explain to him that there was this eleven-volume record of events on the London stage. "Just the thing," he said. "Perfect. Look here, you hop on a plane and come out and see me and we'll work this thing out. Same problem as the big bibliography I've been doing for Colorado University. Only let me warn you. Be sure to get enough money. Don't get halfway through and run out of money."

All that was five years before I got the job, let alone the money, so I never did hop the plane. I wrote a letter, instead, which dropped into a void. As I would learn, face to face or telephone was the only mode of communication among computer men. I don't know when I found out that Benster's project at the University of Colorado was Lewis Sawin's Automated Bibliography of American Literature. But I have a record of the fact that three days after receiving Dean Stone's invitation I was on the telephone to Lewis Sawin. I thought I had to get a few concrete ideas from someone who had been there, before putting together a proposal for the pilot project.

"Ah yes," said Sawin. "That project is on the shelf, you know. Our funds dried up." Having heard Benster cry, "Follow copy," I was curious about the bibliography's method of input. I trusted they had not used the keypunch? No, they certainly had not; they had used a Duramatic typewriter, actually an IBM bouncing ball machine that punched a paper tape. Lewis offered to make the project's programs available to me. They had been advised to do them in a universal "algorithmic" style, so that they could be used on any computer and translated easily into any computer language. I gratefully accepted his offer. Before hanging up, Lewis gave me some advice that has resounded ever since in the corridors of my memory. "Foundations are going sour on computer projects that don't pan out. Make sure your goals are attainable. At all costs get results."

Such advice was academic unless we had funds to go ahead with. I knew I would need a half-year's salary for me, a year's salary for a programmer, the price of a good piece of *The London Stage* in machine-readable form, and something for supplies and expenses. I guessed it would come to about $40,000. Dean Stone was optimistic about getting help from the National Endowment for the Humanities, but only on a matching basis. If we raised half of the money, they would give us the other half. Where would our half come from? Could we get it in time to start next fall?

During the next academic year I could work on the project. The year after that I was due for a sabbatical in England. I could not postpone my leave another year without jeopardizing my children's education. My eldest daughter would be doing her final year in college, a bad year to do abroad, and my eldest son would be a freshman at college, another bad year to do abroad. My younger son and daughter were not in such delicate positions, but we'd been planning on England ever since the last sabbatical, and there would be grave disappointment if we had to wait another year. So, if it was to be at all, the pilot project had to be next year. After the sabbatical could come the project proper. Dean Stone thought that the lapse would help our chances of raising funds by allowing for a more deliberate approach. Could we get enough money to proceed next September? I determined to visit my parents in Boston and drop in on Dean Stone in New York with this question on the way back.

When one imagines developing a mechanism for instantly finding out whether Mrs. Mirthwit is or is not the name of a character in an 18th century play, one does not imagine that a large part of his time will be occupied with financial affairs. But, beginning with this trip, bread and butter became my frequent errand. Before this tale was ended, I would write four grant proposals averaging thirty pages each, make a grant report of ten pages, compile seven budgets, work out nine contracts, scrutinize twenty-four monthly accounts, and pay countless bills. And would pursue numerous other activities not entirely disinterested, undertaken at least partly with a view to developing public confidence and support, such as placing eleven announcements in as many journals, mailing out two newsletters (circulation 175), reporting to four Advisory Board meetings in four cities, giving three papers at two conferences, published as four articles, and helping organize one seminar at a convention. My research has not been entirely pure.

The big question I carried with me to Washington Square was, "How soon will we know we can go ahead?" The question was, of course, unanswerable. Only those with money to give could tell. Dean Stone and I put together, during an afternoon and evening, our first proposal to the National Endowment for the Humanities, based on my piloting concept and an earlier plan of his. This plan had collapsed at the demise of the undertaking body, an organization called bravely The Institute for Computer Research in the Humanities at New York University—an Ozymandias for all computing humanists to look on and despair. Dean Stone, undaunted, would carry our proposal to Washington within the week. But even if the Endowment reacted positively, as he expected, we would still not have one penny unless we raised one ourselves, in which case we would have two. Dean Stone would start "beating the bushes" immediately. He had a great many prospects in mind.

Flying back to Appleton the next day, I realized that I was like a man who had been promised a job on the condition that an employer could be found. By June the situation was still "iffy." The Endowment had committed itself to matching anything up to $20,000, but none of the foundations Dean Stone had approached could decide for us or against us until this or that board or committee met on such and such a far off date. He had frequently urged me to "get Lawrence into the fund-raising act," and I began to think that this might be a way of getting something settled. I asked President Smith, "What if we established here a Lawrence University Center for Theatre Information (any substantial donor can replace "Lawrence University" with his own name), consisting of *The London Stage* and other basic theatrical reference works. Would Lawrence be interested in seeking funds for such a thing?" On the condition that the information bank became the property of Lawrence, he favored the idea. I therefore composed my second grant proposal, in three grand phases—pilot, completion, expansion.

The Southern Illinois University Press, who held the copyright of *The London Stage*, was the only party who could prevent us from using the information we put into our computer. I therefore made my first venture into the field of contract writing:

AGREEMENT

Southern Illinois University Press and Lawrence University

Southern Illinois University Press grants Lawrence University exclusive rights to produce and maintain any computer-readable form of *The London Stage, 1660–1800*, to be used for the purpose of mechanical information retrieval as an aid to scholarly research; in return for this privilege Lawrence agrees to produce and maintain a *London Stage* Information Bank and to make available to any academic researchers any set of information contained therein which is amenable to a mechanical search at a price of no more than Lawrence's cost for each information search.

Much to my surprise, our lawyer and the Press's lawyer found very little to object to. Vernon Sternberg, Director of the Press, made sure that the comprehensive computer-made index, already part of our proposal to the National Endowment for the Humanities, was stipulated. In the extent of my commitments, at least, I was making progress.

———————————

The family spent that summer in my parent's home near Boston, weekending at the New Hampshire lake to which the Schneiders had retreated since I was little. What I mostly remember, however, is sitting soaking wet in a sweltering carrel at Widener Library of Harvard University, day after day, doing information retrieval in the traditional way. The book I had written about comedies popular on the London stage from 1660 to 1730 was finally going to press, and all the footnotes had to be checked for accuracy. As a consequence of my trying to discuss 83 different plays, so many different books were involved that I spent so much time simply gathering in the books from all those acres of stacks piled on stacks that I made very little headway with the footnotes. To save the day, my wife volunteered as a stack boy. Kay, for that is her name, also maintained diplomatic relations between me and the German stack clerk, who was finding a great deal to disapprove of in the accuracy with which I made out reservation cards. The library's computer, he explained to me through her, would be unable to deal with the cards unless I mended my ways. One day a library guard referred to us as "intellectuals." Kay laughed, I thought a bit too hard, at this, after such intimate experience with the work that intellectuals do. With her chasing the books, we got done in a week and made the publisher's deadline. The episode dramatized, all the same, how a scholar's clerical work multiplies when he deals with a repetitive genre like drama. I became all the more determined to build a *London Stage* Information Bank and liberate theatre historians' wives from endless drudgery.

I now turned my attention to Automatic Information Retrieval. Widener Library, one of the seven largest in the world, had no more than a dozen books on the subject, half of which were really books on library science. The periodical collection contained none of the basic computer journals, not even *Communications of the Association for Computing Machinery* and its satellites, *Computing Reviews* and *Journal of the ACM. Computer World, Datamation,* and the other business-oriented magazines were missing, too. This dearth of material on computers was all the more surprising because Widener Library was itself nationally famous for its own efficient system of keeping track of books by computer. To read *Computing Reviews* at Harvard, it was necessary to travel half a mile north of Widener, past Sanders Theatre, to one of the physics buildings in the green lane across from the glass flowers, climb four flights of staircases smelling of science, past the usual dedicatory plaques and memorial sculptures, past glass cases full of souvenirs of someone's late 19th century expedition to Peru, past the usual inoperative water clock and historic x-ray tube, to a small just-renovated science library, so little known and little used that you didn't even have to show a pass. If you knew where it was you were authorized to use it.

When it did not concern itself with the obvious, information retrieval was a very hard subject. Most of it focussed on the structure of the information in the computer's memory. I learned that a piece of information might have an "address," like a house, that you could have "pointers" at an address leading to related facts, like an owner's name, stored elsewhere, and his annual income, stored elsewhere. These facts, though randomly scattered in memory, were said to be "chained." The point of all this was to "optimize search efficiency" and save valuable computer time. There were few lucid moments in the week or so I devoted to reading up on information retrieval, but I gathered that great savings in search time could be made by the arrangement of items in one's file, and that because storage space was always cheaper than search time, wasteful uses of space (like three different arrangements of one set of data) were preferable to wasteful search routines.

I concluded that what I wanted was a series of very long IBM cards, each card recording the performance of a role in a play at a theatre on a date. If each kind of item always occurred in the same slot, cubbyhole, or "field," as they called it, on the card, then I could search for any item in its field, and the rest of the facts about the performance would be chained to it by the card. This was the way it had worked in my coquette-prude project. Only to cram all this information on a card, it had been necessary to choose each play title from a fixed table of three-letter abbreviations and to choose all role and actor names from a table of six-letter abbreviations. Charles Lord had to look up or remember every abbreviation whenever it occurred. This meant also that the output was gibberish to anyone unfamiliar with the abbreviations. Although it is nice to have everything on a solid unit of paper that you can hold in your hand, the necessity of abstracting and coding in order to squeeze a record onto a card is one big reason why I don't like cards. The very long IBM card on which I imagined that my units of data could be stored in memory could have fixed fields or it could have fields of variable length, but the fields must be long enough to contain every name and title in full. If I could help it, I decided that there would be no coding or abbreviation of items of input or output. This was the philosophy of "English in and English out" proposed by Kraft and echoed by Benster at that conference at Purdue.

I was beginning to get my bearings, but in order to locate if possible a few more fixed points in a world still full of if's and maybe's, I decided to complete the summer by attending a convention of the Association for Computing Machinery at the New York Hilton that I had read about on the top floor of the physics building. Both SIGIR and SIGLASH—i.e., Special Interest Group in Information Retrieval and Special Interest Group in Language Arts, Social Sciences, and Humanities—were having meetings; there would be a special session on "humanities applications." I was horrified at the price. Just to register cost $75, not including room and board. I was beginning to realize that the computer milieu operated on an entirely different scale of values from the academic world, where professional activities generally cost sums like $18 or $26. In the computer magazines price tags like $98,750 or $4950 were common enough; they treated thousands of dollars the way supermarkets treat dollars; and hundreds were their nickels and dimes.

I found the New York Hilton to be a super motel in structure as well as in taste. The motel and the computer have developed side by side, perhaps even hand in hand. I don't think I have ever seen a curlicue on a piece of computer hardware. Perhaps because of the mechanical atmosphere or perhaps because the price was too high, only twelve people attended the session on humanities applications. It consisted, moreover, of "state of the art" articles that would appear in a few weeks in *Computers and the*

Humanities. Nor were the authors themselves in attendance to answer questions. Their papers were read for
them by local proxies to save them the trouble of traveling.
Not even the advertised chairman was there. I have sensed
that space on computer conference programs and in computer journals is less at a premium than it is in the professional outlets of the older disciplines. SIGIR I had not
joined so I missed their meeting. But SIGLASH was
attended by only seven people, of whom four were in-
coming or outgoing officers. The principal activities were administrative and social. I was in the process of discovering
that humanistic computing was a cloud no bigger than a
man's hand.

The exhibits, however, were interesting—especially
one. I pass by the computer art, the junior high school
computing whiz kids, the automatic heart disease diagnoser,
the computerized kitchen, and the chess tournament between five computers. My attention fixed on Meade Data
Central's demonstration of a generalized information system. There I saw a man sitting before a TV screen with a
keyboard similar to the ones at the Institute of Paper
Chemistry. But the little green letters on the screen spelled
out a contemporary Broadway play, the theatre at which it
was playing, and the time at which the curtain rose.
"What's this?" I asked. He pressed a key and more titles
appeared on the screen. "Oh, I'm just querying our New
York entertainment directory." Needless to say, I stood as if
thunderstruck. "How does it work?" I sputtered. He held
up a calming hand. "You're just in time for our next
demonstration." Forthwith three girls in purple pantsuits
materialized in the booth, which was about the size of a
small livingroom, and began to trade sentences with each
other. It went something like this:

Girl A: Are you having trouble keeping up with the information you need to have to conduct your business

properly? Would you like to have all the facts necessary for making important decisions right at your fingertips?

Girl B: What you need is Meade Data Central's generalized information system, especially designed with you in mind. Meade's system is not on the drawing board but fully operative in several configurations of basic information-handling applications. It is ready now to serve you. [Turning to girl C, seated at a TV screen] Cathy will now demonstrate one of these applications.

They gestured as they spoke, as if they performed for an audience of thousands. My impulse was to look behind to see who they were addressing. But except for a casual glancer or two, I was the whole audience. It was so disconcerting to see a commercial in the flesh, and possibly as disconcerting to the commercial, that I learned little from Cathy's demonstration, which had something to do with the statutes of the state of Ohio.

As one of the youths in the booth, who turned out to be a marketing official of the firm, explained to me later, these terminals at the Hilton were connected by long distance telephone lines to Meade's computer in Dayton, Ohio, where the statutes of the state resided on a random access disk storage device. He showed me that one could call up statutes pertaining to a topic by searching for words associated with the topic. For instance, if we were interested in knife murders, we could search for statutes containing the word "knife." The system worked like John Bachhuber's at the Institute of Paper Chemistry, except that instead of searching for key words that abstractors had assigned to the documents, Meade searched for actual words in the document.

I wondered whether Meade's system could compile a list of the actors who played Romeo, giving the date and theatre of each performance. I told the young man my story about eleven volumes of performances on London stages from 1660 to 1800 that I was to tell hundreds of times in the next year. I thought at first he was going to laugh, but instead he gave me a sort of unbelieving suspicious smile; perhaps he was just a little bit afraid that I was putting him on. I was to see this look hundreds of times —almost as many times as I told my story—on the faces of members of the computer fraternity. For despite their universal belief that computer methods will ease every mortal's load, they find it hard to believe that a sane person would want to know who played Romeo in the 18th century. When, indeed, on silver or TV screen did a theatre historian ever hold forth? The media do not know of his existence, so how can he be said to exist?

Although I do not believe that I ever convinced the people at Meade Data that I was real, I truly believed that Meade was real. They were a subsidiary of Meade Paper, of which I had heard. It looked as though their system might work for *The London Stage*. The burning question of course was, "How much?" The young men would get their heads together and let me know the next day, after talking to one of their technologists. "About $26,000," was their eventual quotation, accompanied, I thought, by stifled mirth. That included the retrieval system and data capture. There would also be a nominal charge for every query and for telephone connection to Dayton. "Only that much?" I asked. Perhaps a moment of truth came then, because I knew they knew that *The London Stage* contained 8026 pages, and I knew that they had to make a living, pay for that computer in Dayton, and Girls A, B, and C. We both knew that just to type *The London Stage* would cost nearly $26,000. But I think they had expected to demolish me with that figure. Now it was my turn to register disbelief. Still, it was the first dollar figure I'd heard, and it came from a commercial house. It must be, then, a point to pilot by.

Before returning to Appleton, I visited Richard Golden in the computer facility of the City University of New York at Fifth Avenue and 42nd Street. Richard was consultant on information retrieval for the American Council of Learned Societies, a principal source of funds for academic research in disciplines other than science. I found him to be young, dark, slender, serious, soft-voiced, and fast-talking, as if his output was striving desperately to keep up with his extremely fast central processor. With lightning speed he described his work, a generalized index formatting system for printing any kind of index by computer, and went on to describe my work, which he instantly and perfectly comprehended. He touched upon the MT/ST, interactive terminals, commercial information services, and the structure of data bases, but he came back always to what he referred to as "syntactic analysis." All I could think of was identifying parts of speech and diagramming sentences; I couldn't quite see what this might have to do with computing. "The first thing you have to do is sit down and describe that data base, and you have to keep at it and at it until you've got it right. What each unit consists of, what repeats, what doesn't repeat, what has to be there, what may or may not be there. This you have to do before you can write programs that work."

So, by the end of the summer of 1970 I thought I knew five things: English in and English out. Follow copy. Get results. Optimize data structure to maximize search efficiency. Analyze the syntax. I did not know whether Meade Data could answer my needs.

Labor Day, mustering time for academic families, found us back home ready to start school. Appleton, Wisconsin, in Green Bay Packerland on the Fox River, 200 miles north of Chicago, not far from Little Chute, Grand Chute, Lake Butte des Morts, Oshkosh, Kaukauna, Neenah, Menasha, and Combined Locks, is famous as the home of

Houdini, Edna Ferber, and Joseph R. McCarthy. Law-rence University is a classic midwest coeducational liberal arts college, called a university to account for the fact that as of 1964 it includes Milwaukee-Downer College for Women. It was founded in 1850 with a gift of $10,000 from the textile magnate Amos Lawrence, whose wife was Sarah Appleton, the gift to be matched by Methodists in the Territory of Wisconsin. This same Amos Lawrence was the man who had thought of importing English female textile workers to Massachusetts so that he could improve them morally and intellectually with his educational system while his extremely profitable mills benefitted from their skilled labor. Lawrence College was a similarly two-edged venture, uplifting the region while increasing the rent of the big piece of Wisconsin territory that he had bought as an investment. Perhaps because of their New England connections, the arrangement of the mills on the Fox River at Appleton, Neenah, and Menasha suggests the mills on the Merrimack at Nashua, Lowell, Lawrence, and Haver-hill, although paper is the Fox Valley's business instead of textiles. Lawrence is famous as the college where Henry Wriston, Nathan Pusey, Douglas Knight, and Curtis Tarr were presidents before they became, respectively, presidents of Brown, Harvard, Duke, and Assistant Secretary of State. As textiles began it, paper has carried it on, paper men have composed its board of trustees, and paper money has bailed it out of jams. Thus it is that when the winds blow foul from the mills and the sulphides and sulphites burden the air, one is sure to hear the remark, said to be Nathan Pusey's, to the effect that it is the smell of money and that when it stops Lawrence will stop.

As of Labor Day 1970, though, no winds good or ill had blown any dollars into the coffers of the *London Stage* Information Bank project. The plan already agreed upon with the English department was that if the money materialized, I would teach the three courses comprising a half-load at the rate of one course first term, no course second term, and two courses third term. Unless I handed over the project to someone like Meade, I would need the aid of a full-time programmer. Having quit math forever after a disastrous struggle with calculus in college, I knew that I would be no use to the project in this capacity. If Meade actually were the answer, I could not decide this anyhow without knowing a great deal more about information retrieval than I did at this time. But it seemed to me that Meade's service as now offered would *not* produce the tabulated role histories and actor careers we needed. Ours was probably too special an information base to fit into a general system. If in the end, after we had paid $26,000, the system turned out to be unsuitable, it would still be their system to be adjusted at their pleasure. Probably the text could be converted to computer tape for less than $26,000. There was nothing for it but to start out on our own.

I couldn't very well invite a programmer to come without offering him at least an academic year's work. A programmer's salary and a bit for a machine-readable sample were essential. News now came that the Billy Rose Foundation, created by the will of that Broadway impresario who gave the world the Aquacade, starring Eleanor Holm Jarrett, later Mrs. Rose, would almost certainly contribute a sum large enough, when matched by funds from the Endowment, to supply this bare minimum. On the strength of this promise I decided to look for a programmer and start work in earnest. It was like drawing to an inside straight.

In the search for a programmer I made out job descriptions headed, "Wanted: programmer for the *London Stage* Project," to computer people wherever I knew that a considerable number of non-scientists were involved in computing. I called Sally Sedelow, who had just moved out to the University of Kansas from the University of North Carolina at Chapel Hill. She thought of several prospects, but a fellow named Will Daland, who had sat next to her in a logic class at North Carolina and was about to receive a B.S. in computer science, seemed the most likely. Enquiries revealed that he was interested; that he'd spent some of his high school years in Brazil, where his father, a professor of political science with origins in Wisconsin, was doing research; that his hobby was the simulation by computer of human nerve processes, on which he'd done grant-supported research as an undergraduate; that he had majored with success in computer science; that he'd programmed for a medical research team and was just now completing work with a psychometric laboratory. Those for whom he had worked at Chapel Hill were unanimous in their opinion that he was a good programmer; it was said that he worked far into the night. Most important, he was a specialist in PL/1 (Programming Language One), one of the languages by which one could communicate with the computer at the Institute of Paper Chemistry and said to be excellent for handling text. As the end of the month approached, he was still the best candidate, so I offered him the job beginning on the first of October, and he took it.

The day before he arrived on campus, I had word that the American Council of Learned Societies would donate $12,500 to the project, $5000 for itself and $7500 for United States Steel, for whom they were agent. However, since the National Endowment for the Humanities had a rule that they would not match other government money and since ACLS was partly supported by the Endowment itself, neither U.S. Steel's contribution nor that of ACLS could be doubled. But Will's salary, at least, was taken care of. I had made my straight.

CHAPTER III

CONCERNING
THE SPECS

Will Daland, the Programmer/Analyst, arrives. Some account of The London Stage, 1660–1800. *The first Advisory Board meeting. The Author's correspondence, &c., with Brüder Rosenbaum about Monotype Spools. His Dialogues with Will. The Geography of* The London Stage *and the first edition of the Specs.*

When he appeared that first morning on my office doorstep, I saw that Will was a squarely built, medium-height, blue-eyed, sandy-haired fellow, wearing a light-blue windbreaker, wrinkled tan trousers, and worn-out light-gray suede moccasin-type shoes. He had a forelock like Skeezix and a big brain-dome behind it. We shook hands and I hoped he'd had a good trip. He considered the proposition for a moment before saying, "Yes, fairly good." The main thing, he said, was for me to tell him exactly what I wanted. I described in considerable detail, using a volume of *The London Stage* and a blackboard, the idea of tabulating role-histories and actors' careers by sorting records consisting of a performance of a role by an actor at a theatre on a date. That was how we would deal with cast lists.

For comments and other leftover information I thought we wanted some kind of program like John Bachhuber's for collecting items by key words assigned to them or like Meade Data's for finding passages containing any given word. Also, we had to make some sort of an index for the Southern Illinois University Press. Will said, "It's a good idea to have things like this in writing. To prevent mix-ups." The firmness with which he said the words suggested a second level of meaning: "Programmer not responsible for errors caused by employer's ambiguity or failure to specify." This was fair enough.

Will's first job was to get acquainted with the local system, to find out what resources were available and how they might best be used. Lawrence owned an old IBM 1620 machine, used mainly for teaching programming and for administrative jobs like payrolls and grades. It was too slow for our purposes. The IBM 360 at the Institute of Paper Chemistry, Will explained to me, could operate in three modes or "systems," depending on which was "up" at the time. A computer's "system" is the set of programs by which it administers itself, routes work, uses its various input and output devices, and records accounting information. The simplest system of the Institute's 360 was called "OS," signifying somewhat pretentiously "Operating System," in which one user did one job at a time with the whole computer. OS was used for big jobs requiring lots of "core storage," or computer memory, and lots of input-output capacity. This 360 could store 128,000 characters, about half of this book, in its core memory. The second mode or system of the 360 was RAX, meaning "Remote Access System." For four hours a day the 360 was set up to process simultaneously jobs entered from the Institute's six TV-screen cathode ray tube terminals. Although it seems to each user that he has the whole machine, actually the computer visits each terminal in rotation quickly doing a little bit of work at each visit. This method of serving more than one terminal at a time is called "time-sharing," and it is the way third (next-to-last) generation computers make up for waste of their precious time caused by the fact that they can process data many times faster than any reading or writing machine can supply it or report the results. The solution is to plug six, eight, ten, dozens, or hundreds of terminals into the computer in such a way that while it's waiting for one to give or take, it can go on to the next. The third mode of the 360 was PS, which also enabled one person to use the whole computer for special purposes not important to us. Will spent a few days figuring out RAX, it being the element of the new environment most foreign to him. He reported that because it operates in FORTRAN and lacks a full upper and lower case character set it would be of limited use to us, if any. Our work would be done in PL/1, with the computer in OS mode.

Only a week after Will arrived, we were due in Carbondale, Illinois, to help celebrate the completion of the eleven volumes of *The London Stage*, after thirty-five years of work, and to report to our first Advisory Board meeting. An Advisory Board consisting of the editors and publisher of *The London Stage* with Dean Stone as Chairman had been written into the application to the Endowment, and it was to this group that I was ultimately responsible.

Why it is that civilizations treasure the remains of their past and strive to keep them as neatly on file as possible each reader may answer for himself. But the history of the theatre is at least as fascinating to some as the history of Parliament, warfare, baseball, or furniture is to others. The period naturally bounded by the Restoration in 1660 and somewhat arbitrarily bounded at 1800 is truly the most interesting period in English stage history simply because this is the first period for which we have complete records of performances. Prior to 1660 stage history is a most difficult art. During the Restoration and 18th century there are good new plays by Congreve, Wycherley, Farquhar, Gay, Steele, Goldsmith, and Sheridan; good old plays whose theatrical fortunes and vicissitudes are for the first time well recorded, by Shakespeare, Beaumont and Fletcher, and Ben Jonson; great French plays by Molière and Racine in English versions; theatrical music by Purcell, Bach, Handel, and Mozart; performers like Ann Bracegirdle, Nell Gwyn, Peg Woffington, Sarah Siddons, William Betterton, Robert Wilkes, David Garrick, and John Kemble.

The attempt to compile an account of performances on the London stage during the 18th century had begun almost as soon as the century was over. It was John Genest who first saw the value of sorting out all this stage history and publishing it as a service to lovers of Hamlet or Lord Foppington, Bartholomew Fair or Drury Lane, Bracegirdle or Garrick, *The Way of the World*, *The Beggar's Opera*, or *The School for Scandal*. By 1832 he had published a good part of the record in ten volumes. He did his work so well that it was not until the first half of the 20th century, when English studies burgeoned all over the United States, that anyone saw fit to improve upon his work. Then in the thirties a group of Harvard Ph.D.'s led by William van Lennep and George Winchester Stone, Jr., decided that a new work incorporating new evidence now available had to be compiled. When they had finished they hoped it could be said that any information on the subject that they had not included did not exist.

Van Lennep was a great collector of theatrical relics and builder of the Harvard Theatre Collection. Stone was a student of Shakespeare's fortunes on the 18th century stage, especially in the hands of Garrick. They were joined by Emmett L. Avery, an expert on Congreve, by Arthur H. Scouten, a historian of the farce, and by Charles Beecher Hogan, a Yale scholar who had published a complete record of Shakespeare's plays on the 18th century stage. Avery began compiling materials on Congreve in 1932. Van Lennep and Stone began to revise Genest in 1935. The American Philosophical Society, the American Council of Learned Societies, and the Guggenheim Foundation; the Universities of New York, Pennsylvania, George Washington, and Washington State; and the Folger and Huntington Libraries contributed funds to the enterprise. The five editors ransacked the British and the Victoria and Albert Museums in London; the Harvard, Folger, Huntington, Newberry, and thirteen other libraries in the United States. They acknowledge over two hundred basic sources, used hundreds of others, and looked at thousands. In addition to this, van Lennep was curator of the Harvard Theatre Collection; Stone was the executive secretary of the Modern Language Association of America and Dean of the Graduate School of Arts and Sciences at New York University; Scouten and Avery were professors of English at Pennsylvania and Washington State; and Hogan was a research fellow at Yale. In 1960 the first part was published and in 1970, thirty-five years after van Lennep and Stone conceived of the work, the last volume was published. Van Lennep, who died in 1962, never saw the full set on a shelf.

And now, in October 1970, Vernon Sternberg, the energetic and imaginative director of the Southern Illinois University Press and himself a theatre historian, was putting on a gala celebration of the completion of the task. It featured a command performance of the four editors by particular desire of the Carbondale intelligentsia and a major lecture by Professor Harry Levin of Harvard, as well as a banquet and a reception. Our first Advisory Board meeting was sandwiched in between these festivities.

At this meeting Will and I hoped we could settle three questions, without firm answers to which it was proving quite difficult to talk fruitfully of programming. One was what kind of comprehensive index to plan for Vernon to publish as a companion to the completed volumes—whether of names only, or names and titles, or names, titles, and subjects. The second was whether, since the facts were filed both by date and by page in the source, we should index the material by page or date. I was all for dates, because with as many as fifteen performances on a page these would be more precise, but Will didn't care which so long as we knew. The third question was whether we would "rekey" (type or keypunch) the text in order to get it in a machine-readable form or whether we could somehow convert paper spools of coded paper ribbon that had driven the automatic type-setting machines used in printing *The London Stage*.

I had already learned in my travels that most books published today actually pass through a machine-readable version on the way to the printing press. Therefore most new books could be stored for the computer at a negligible cost. But coded paper tape used for printing is perishable and is usually discarded. I had heard rumors to the effect that someone, realizing that the work was probably destined for the computer, had taken measures to see that the printers saved the machine-readable by-product of printing *The London Stage*, but four of the five parts had been set before the saving commenced. Hence, only a month after receiving Dean Stone's invitation to undertake the project, I had written to Vernon asking how much of *The London Stage* was available on punched paper tape. A few days later I had an answer: "*The London Stage* was composed in Vienna on English Monotype. When we started the project the paper used for Monotype tape was fragile, and was not saved. I do not know what is recoverable—chances are, none, but I have written to find out. I will let you know when I find out. Once again, I suggest you count on none."

So I gave up all hope of machine-readable tapes for *The London Stage*. But on July 9th I received word from Vernon that "The tapes, all 300 of them, are available at $3/tape." All the tapes had been saved? or, All the tapes that are saved are available? $3 \times 300 = \$900$. This would be cheap perhaps for the whole text, but expensive for a part. I expressed some bewilderment and suggested that perhaps Vernon should get a sample as fast as he could. On August 15th he wrote, "All the tapes for all the volumes are available," and that when he had a firm order from me he would order a sample from Vienna. I forthwith wrote a firm order, and we were still waiting for a response from Austria when we assembled in the president's Meeting Room at Southern Illinois University for our first Advisory Board meeting. Vernon now had word that the printers still had 429 reels of tape for Part 2. This statement seemed incompatible with the notion that "all 300" meant "all of *The London Stage*," but for the moment I let that pass.

Vernon had made it clear to me that the tape would be full of errors that had since been corrected in galleys and page proofs. So correcting the text after conversion to the computer would have to be considered as part of the cost of using the Vienna tapes. But since we would at any rate have to write a program for correcting text after entry, there would be no extra programming. Moreover, if the editors had saved their galley and page proofs, we could simply transfer their corrections to our converted tapes. A lot would depend on whether the editors had saved their proofs. In fact, we discovered at the Advisory Board meeting that, with the typical packrat instinct of scholars and antiquarians everywhere, they had done so. I now saw no obstacle to conversion of printers' tapes, although Vernon, more experienced in the vicissitudes of text-processing than I, shook his head dubiously.

The questions about what kind of index to compile took up more of our time. The editors had, after thirty-five years, made up their minds about what kind of index they preferred. It would be the traditional index to page numbers. Will and I could not entirely agree. But, they argued, scholars expect an index to page numbers, and page numbers it therefore must be. I pointed out that it would be easier to find an item in the span of text governed by a date than in that governed by a page. Also, what was to be done about all those items in all those entries where the editors had simply given a previous date on which that cast could be found? Suppose "Garrick" is actually associated with a performance on November 18th but is noticed merely under the reference "Hamlet. As 22 Sept." The program we envisioned would ferret out the previous performance and record both Garrick and his role on November 18th. But with as many as thirty such references on a page, how could the user of the index knowing only the page number ever find out under which entry or entries Garrick was hiding? Besides, dates were actual information, pages were not. An index entry of an actor's appearances on the London stage by date would immediately give an idea of that actor's stage career, showing at a glance the fat and lean years, the gaps, the beginnings and endings. The Board saw what I meant but thought a conventional index best for the audience intended. I did not belabor the point, believing as I did that computers were too often justly accused of being uselessly disruptive of accustomed ways of doing things.

What would the index consist of? The editors and Vernon had already decided that the index must be limited to names and titles.

The Board at this time felt it advisable to expand itself so as to include notable English stage historians and other important Americans. It was agreed that Dean Stone would invite Professor Allardyce Nicoll, president of the Society for Theatre Research, London, an author of basic books on London stage history; Miss Sybil Rosenfeld, secretary of the same society and for many years editor of *Theatre Notebook*, its principal publication; Professor Cecil Price, of Swansea University, Wales, the leading authority on the dramatist Richard Brinsley Sheridan; Professors Philip Highfill and Kalman Burnim, of George Washington and Tufts, compilers of a biographical dictionary of actors and actresses; Father Carl Stratman, of Loyola of Chicago, editor of the journal *Restoration and Eighteenth Century Theatre Research* and prolific compiler of dramatic bibliographies, particularly one on the English stage, 1660–1800; and Professor John Robinson of Nebraska, compiler with James Arnott of Glasgow of a bibliography of English theatrical literature from the beginnings to 1900. After setting the time of the next meeting to coincide with the annual meeting of the Modern Language Association between Christmas and the New Year, we adjourned for lunch after a meeting of about two hours.

Will and I drove back to Appleton across the endless prairie of Illinois watching the grain elevators go by and thinking that our work was becoming more complicated. Indexing by pages would not relieve us of filing everything by date, too. The basic unit of data remained in fact a performance at one theatre on one day, and no responsible retrieval system could ignore this. And conversion of Monotype tape was now a real possibility, bringing the Viennese printers and some machine for converting punches in paper to magnetic bits on computer tape into the ever more cluttered picture. Worse, if only part of *The London Stage* had been saved on tape we would find ourselves using two different methods of entry.

Awaiting our return in Appleton was a nubbly package that might have contained a dozen heads of lettuce, loosely wrapped, except that it was too light. It came from Chanticleer Press, 424 Madison Avenue, New York. In it were what looked like thirteen rolls of toilet paper but with a hard grey-green surface, and perforated edges. They were filled with what looked like little wormholes. In the package was a letter from Emma Staffelbach saying, "Mr. Vernon Sternberg asked us to send you the enclosed 13 reels of Monotype tape London Stage, Part 2." Who was Emma Staffelbach? Some of the mystery was cleared up by another message, stuffed in among the rolls of paper, to Miss Staffelbach but apparently never reaching her, from T. Schmutzer, Brüder Rosenbaum, Margaretenstrasse 94, Wien, that read as follows: "In reply to Mr. Steiner of August 26, 1970, we are sending you today via Angerer 13 reels Part V, Volume 2, of the years 1784–85 . . . years 1700–1729 of Part IV not kept here anymore."

No wonder it took so long for Vernon to get an answer about Monotype reels with such a long chain of people between him and the printer. I could see Emma and Mr. Steiner, toiling in back rooms on Madison Avenue over great neatly piled stacks of unanswered mail, Emma with gold-rimmed spectacles and blond braids pinned up and worn as a crown, Herr Steiner a bit stout and florid—in charge of course but in shirt sleeves with arm bands. They had both come to realize he wouldn't do for her. But what about Angerer the courier, tall and thin, with his shiny, slick, black Peter Lorre hair and his insinuating looks, always coming and going? It was as impossible for me to imagine these unknown modes of being as it was for them to imagine me using these tapes in any sensible way.

Emma had written, "We would like to advise you that it is quite possible that the tape does not run consecutively, since it might have been prepared by more than one operator. Also please note, that the page numbers cannot be determined because they were only introduced after the page make-up was prepared. We hope that these limitations will still make it possible to make good use of the material." These objections were trivial, I thought, compared with the alternative of retyping every letter of the whole text.

What Emma and Mr. Steiner couldn't seem to tell me but what I had to know was how much of the text was available. It didn't make sense to set up an elaborate conversion process for a little bit of text. My information to date was inconclusive and contradictory.

Ca. 1967 (rumor): Part 5 available.

20 May 1970: No tapes available.

25 June 1970: "All 300" available.

12 August 1970: "All tapes for all volumes" available.

17 August 1970: I order a tape "preferably from Part 2 or 3."

21 August 1970 (Vernon): "Have ordered you a tape."

25 September 1970 (Schmutzer to Emma): "Sending you today . . . 13 reels Part V Volume 2. . . . Years 1700–1729 of Part IV not kept here anymore."

5 October 1970 (Emma to me): "Mr. Sternberg has asked us to send you 13 reels of Part 2."

12 October 1970 (Advisory Board Meeting): 429 reels for Part 2 available.

14 October 1970 (on hand Appleton): 13 reels of something.

It was like that game we used to play at the Thanksgiving table, in which one person whispered a message into the ear of his neighbor, and it was passed this way all around the table to see what astonishing permutation of the original would come through. But a bit more came through to me than Emma realized, distracted as she was by Angerer. The original rumor that Brüder Rosenbaum had saved all tapes for the last part (5) was correct. When Vernon wrote that no tapes were available, he meant "I doubt very much that the tapes we asked them to save so long ago are still in readable condition, even if they have been kept." When he wrote that "all 300" were available, he was probably repeating what Brüder Rosenbaum told T. Schmutzer to tell Angerer to tell Mr. Steiner to tell Emma to tell him. He interpreted their "all 300" to mean all tapes for all volumes, bypassing the possibility that Brüder Rosenbaum really meant "We still have all 300 that we saved," and he had forgotten, moreover, that four volumes had been published before he, for it must have been he, ever asked Emma to ask Mr. Steiner to ask Angerer to ask T. Schmutzer to ask Brüder Rosenbaum to save any tapes whatsoever. I ordered a tape from Part 2 or 3 to test my hypothesis that Vernon had forgot. And Herr Schmutzer indeed received the message that I wanted something from Part 2, because when he said "1700–1729 of

Part IV are not kept here anymore," he meant "1700–1729 of Part II," which part does actually contain years 1700–1729. Herr Schmutzer, of course, was trying to explain why he did not send anything from Part 2 or 3 which he knew from my order to Vernon that I wanted. Emma's assertion that she was sending me tapes from Part 2 which she, too, by now should know were not kept at Brüder Rosenbaum's anymore was based on her beautiful faith that what Brüder Rosenbaum's customers order, Brüder Rosenbaum deliver. If my answer to my original question, "How much of *The London Stage* is saved on paper tape?" was indeed "All of Part 5," one could now make sense of T. Schmutzer's statement that he had sent "13 reels of Part V, Volume 2, of the years 1784–85." He meant, of course, "Part 5, Volume II, season of 1784–85 complete in 13 reels," forgetting like everyone else who gets embroiled in *The London Stage* whether it is the volumes or the parts that have the Roman numerals. The clincher was that the season of 1784–85 is in 5, II, and by a simple proportion, the one season 1784–85 is to the 25 seasons of part 5 as 13 is to 325. This figure fell close to the "all 300" mentioned in the first place. Everything began to add up.

Turning to the question of how these giant reels of paper tape could be converted to computer tape we encountered new problems. I had seen ticker tape; I had seen teletype tape. Some computers used teletype tape in place of punch cards but this tape was four or five times as wide and very sparsely punched. I could not imagine how this "English Monotype" tape communicated between the compositor and the typesetting machine. So one day soon after the thirteen tapes had arrived, acting on a hint from Win Stone, to the effect that the *Publications of The Modern Language Association* were printed practically next door to us in Monotype by Banta Press, Will and I

took a reel over to the plant in Menasha, where I was introduced to Dave Abraham, chief of the Monotype composing room and Banta's expert on the process. What we
wanted to know was the secret code of the tape. Dave
explained everything about font styles and sizes, the problem
of justification (making the lines come out even), and
character sets; he carefully studied our copy of *The London
Stage*, measured the characters up and down and right and
left, and discovered that the Austrians used a size of type
never seen in the United States. He kept coming back to
the difficulty one would have in discovering and correcting
any unrecorded changes that the printers had made in the
"matrix plan." He showed us how tapes were punched on
the compositor, a typewriter with about 196 keys. Could
we perhaps look at the typesetting machine?

Dave took us to another room full of clanking machines
that were molding and putting type in galleys at a rate of
one piece of type for every three clanks and about nine
clanks per second. Dave explained that the machine finds
out which character to pick, mold, and set from 31 thin
copper tubes in a row going from the paper tape reader to
the picking device. The paper reels unroll one notch at a
time, about one-eighth of an inch. The open ends of the
tubes press against 31 positions in a row across the paper
tape. If there is a hole in the paper in front of any tube's
mouth, compressed air on the other side of the paper tape
shoots through the hole and through the tube to a piston at
the other end. Because the characters are kept in a matrix
case the way chessmen are set on a chess board, only two
holes in the tape are necessary to locate a character, one
telling how high it is in the matrix and another telling how
far to the right—in mathematical lingo, one giving its
x-coordinate and one its y-coordinate. Holes 1 to 14 give
the x-coordinate and holes 15 to 28 give the y-coordinate.
The other three holes, 29 to 31, tell how wide the spaces

must be to justify the line. 14×14 allows for 196 discrete characters.

The secret of justification is a measuring device on the compositor. When the operator nears the end of the line a register shows him how much space is left, enabling him to calculate and key in the proper justification dimension to be added to the width of the slug carrying each character. The most astonishing but, in the end, obvious thing about the system is how the typesetting machine learns the justification dimension, as it must, before it begins to set the line. The operator simply feeds the tape into the typecasting machine backwards.

When the typecasting machine senses two holes in the paper tape it raises an x and a y piston in the casting section. An arm jams the matrix case against the two pistons as far forward and to the right as it will go. The character desired now covers the type mold. Lead is pumped in; the piece of type is then extracted and carried to its place in the galley. This machine, invented in 1901, is still used in almost the original form to set type all over the world.

The same principle is used to inform computers, except that magnetic pressure takes the place of air pressure. One would have thought, therefore, considering how widespread and ancient the Monotype process is (Penguin books are set in Monotype), that some device for converting it to computer tape would have been invented. Machines have been getting their instructions from holes in paper at least since the player piano was invented. All that is necessary for translating from paper holes to magnetic bits is that there be one discrete code in the magnetic medium for every discrete code in the paper medium: any computer with 196 codes can theoretically read Monotype code. Our computer at the Institute could handle 256 codes. A simple program could declare which Monotype code was equivalent to which computer code. Dave knew of a device that converted computer tape to Monotype tape, but none that worked in the opposite direction. He suggested that we write to the sales manager for the Western Hemisphere of the Monotype Corporation at the head office in Redhill, Surrey, England.

Computers could read various other kinds of paper tape as well as various kinds of magnetic tape and punch cards. The main problem, then, was to find a way of converting Monotype tape to one of the media that computers could read; then, if that was not a medium our computer could read, to find a computer that read the foreign medium and could write our kind. The conversion job only had to be done once for all time. Will and I ruled out the possibility of having an electronic 31-channel tape reader made by some engineering firm as too expensive for the amount of data we would have. But if we could somehow convert the compressed-air impulses of the Mono-caster's own reader (supposing that we could borrow or rent one) to electrical impulses by pressure-actuated switches in the tubes or by mechanical switches actuated by the 31 pistons in the machine matrix-positioning apparatus, these electrical impulses could be used to operate a teletype's paper tape punch. The fellow that made apparatus for the Lawrence physics department had one of these. Plenty of computers could read teletype tape and write 360 tape. A third alternative would be to feed electrical impulses from the Monocaster directly into a small computer which would interpret them and convert them to magnetic computer tape. All of these would probably cost high up in the four-figure range. We dropped the matter pending firmer evidence of the amount and quality of tape actually on hand in Vienna.

Meanwhile Will must get to work on programming. But he couldn't very well do it without a sample of machine-readable text to practice on. He wanted to know absolutely and finally and in exhaustive detail exactly what the character of the input to his program would be. Of course, we weren't going to know this until we'd settled on an input medium. And we couldn't decide this without further research. Fortune always dictated that we move on but wouldn't let us scout the terrain ahead.

Having had some experience of projects gone awry because of conceptual differences between programmer and director, Will made it a practice to consult with me almost daily about what he had done, what I wanted done, what he thought we should do, and above all what we should do next. It was a very good idea, because it forced us both to consider our general and necessarily vague ideas of the project's goal against the hard and irreducible facts of implementation, to choose between concrete alternatives, to make irreversible but necessary decisions. The organic structure of *The London Stage* itself, which we must describe before we could analyze it by machine, continually evaded us. To retrieve what was in it we had to know what kinds of things were in it and how these kinds were arranged. It was like Nature itself. We always thought we knew more about it than we actually did.

And so Will appeared daily at my home or office for consultation. Although he had a completely non-random mind, the times of his appearances were random. At least I never discovered their basic law. Many times he looked very sleepy, but I never knew, unless I asked, whether he was just getting up or on his way to bed. He told me once that it was his habit to stay up an hour later every day and get up an hour later the next day, so as to lengthen his waking life. He said it was his custom before going on a visit to stay up later and later for several nights preceding until his bedtime came in the morning. Then instead of wasting the next eight hours sleeping, he wasted them driving and put off that day's sleep until bedtime at his hosts'.

The conditions of a programmer's life seem to foster such habits. Because computers are always busiest in normal working hours, programmers who need their full attention must seek audience in abnormal working hours. Moreover computers have to have artificial climates which are best achieved in windowless chambers. In consequence computer men do not see daylight during working hours and become unconscious of the coming and going of the day and the night. The environment of the computer man is indeed a new instance of *The Wasteland* that T. S. Eliot describes. "Summer surprised us coming over the Starnbergersee. . . . I read much of the night and go south in the winter. . . . In the mountains there you feel free. . . . The hot water at ten, the closed car at four." Modern conveniences desensitize us to equinoctial, diurnal, and meteorological change. Or is it a line from Wordsworth that expressed it first: "Little we have in Nature that is ours."

With Vienna still a question mark, two other ways of getting Will a sample large enough to be representative on which to try out his programs were immediately available to us. We could use the tried and true keypunch or we could look into the MT/ST's that the Institute was using for its computerized paper chemistry abstract service. Will, anxious to get going, advocated putting a girl to work on a keypunch immediately. I hated to get started with cards. I would never forget the days I had spent on my coquette-prude project, sorting 30,000 cards 32 times to get them in alphabetical order by actor and role and in numerical order by date. Once, near the end of a long hard day, I had picked up the wrong box of cards and, before I knew what I was doing, piled it into the sorter and spoiled my whole day's work. Besides putting ourselves in jeopardy of

cards getting lost, mutilated, or out of order, to recognize
upper case with a keypunch we'd have to precede every
capital letter with a dollar sign or some other special
character. Furthermore, with a keypunch it is impossible to
make corrections in the process of typing because you can't
erase holes in cards and every error requires a new card.
To complicate matters, extra errors are fostered by the fact
that a character punched on a card is not even visible to the
typist until she has punched eight more characters. Thus
she can easily lose her place, produce errors she would not
otherwise make, and continue uselessly typing after a card
has been spoiled. Because of its notorious drawbacks, keypunch services "verify" all their work—have another girl
punch the same data and check the two versions mechanically. I had convinced myself that we should "follow copy"
and relieve our typists of such niggling details. Why make
it hard for everyone?

The MT/ST's that John Bachhuber had showed me
last spring have many advantages over the keypunch. During the typing process the typist can actually backspace and
type over a mistake. She can also play back to her keyboard the magnetic tape that she has made and correct it
during transfer to another tape. In addition, any character
on the keyboard can be used as a unique code for the
computer when a "prefix" key is depressed before the
character is struck. The character then prints in red on the
paper, giving a clear indication to the typist that the code
has been properly made. Besides having upper case and
redface, we could choose our character set from any bouncing ball in the IBM catalog. Undoubtedly we could follow
copy better with a Magnetic Tape Selectric Typewriter.

Having these views, I thought we should try the MT/
ST's at the Institute, and Will, though dubious, could
think of no reason why not. Upon inquiry we discovered

that the MT/ST "pool" would be happy to prepare data for us at five dollars per hour per machine per operator, assuming that they could fit the work into lulls in their own business. Fortunately one of these lulls was upon them at present. We made a date to explain how we wanted the text to be typed. Vague talk must now come to an end. What Will referred to evermore as the "Specs" must be arrived at and put in writing.

Early in the dialectic sessions that ensued, thinking of the tremendous job of typing 8000 pages of tightly packed, closely punctuated text, I had misgivings about the MT/ST and yearned wistfully for the Monotype tapes in Vienna. Will assured me that we were better off copying every-thing over again. I didn't see what difference it made. "Well, the Monotype tape doesn't have any delimiters; if we copy the text they can put them in as they go." I wasn't sure what delimiters did. "They de-limit. Tell you where a thing begins and ends." Here began our most common form of debate in which I affirmed the proposition that you could tell where a unit of text began and ended from the way it was punctuated in the original and Will showed me how shortsighted I was.

The remarks that follow are illustrated by the page in facsimile of *The London Stage* shown in Figure 1. A typi-cal entry is the last on the page, referring to *The Jealous Wife*. I insisted, for example, that the computer could identify an actor's name in such an entry because the name would be delimited by a hyphen in front and a semicolon after. It was therefore unnecessary to add any delimiters. "Never?" asked Will. I thought so. "What about the actors in the previous entry? I mean *The Mistake*." "Oh

COMMENT. Mainpiece: Reduc'd to two acts. After which (being particularly desired) will be performed the *New Serenata*, composed by Dr Arne in honour of the late Royal Nuptials.   *Wednesday 17* DL

JUDAS MACCHABAEUS. As 5 March.   CG
MUSIC. As 26 Feb.
COMMENT. By Command of their Majesties.

TANCRED AND SIGISMUNDA. As 24 Sept. 1761, but Tancred – Garrick; Sigismunda – Mrs Cibber; Officers: Scrase, Castle, &c. Also HIGH LIFE BELOW STAIRS. As 8 Sept. 1761.   *Thursday 18* DL
SINGING. Hearts of Oak. [No cast listed, but see 9 Feb.]
COMMENT. Benefit for Mrs Cibber. No Building on Stage. Part of Pit laid into Boxes. Ladies send servants by 3 o'clock.

KING HENRY IV, Part 2. As 18 Jan. Also THE CORONATION. As 13 Nov. 1761.   CG
DANCING. III: *The Pleasures of Spring*, as 12 Feb.
COMMENT. Last time of performing *The Coronation* till Easter Monday.

SAMSON. As 10 March.   *Friday 19* DL
MUSIC. As 5 March.
COMMENT. Oratorio By Desire. "Mrs Pritchard's great demand for places tomorrow night, obliges her to request the Ladies will send their Servants early to prevent any mistakes in placing them."

SEMELE. *Cast not listed.* Parts were: Jupiter, Cadmus (King of Thebes), Athamas (Prince of Boeotia, in love with Semele); Somnus, Apollo, Cupid, Juno, Iris, Semele (Daughter of Cadmus); Ino; Chorus of Priests and Augurs; Chorus of Loves and Zephyrs; Chorus of Nymphs and Swains; Attendants (Larpent MS 43).   CG
MUSIC. As 26 Feb.
COMMENT. This day publish'd *Semele* set to Music by Mr Handel. Price 1s. As it is performed this evening at the Theatre Royal in Covent Garden. Printed for J. & R. Tonson in the Strand.

THE MISTAKE. Principal characters by: Garrick, King, Palmer, Yates, Bransby, Philips, Burton, Blakes, Mrs Clive, Mrs Davies, Mrs Bennet, and Mrs Pritchard. [See parts assigned 22 April.] Also THE OLD MAID. As 14 Nov. 1761, but Harlow, Heartwell, Servant, Trifle omitted.   *Saturday 20* DL
DANCING. End of Play: By Particular Desire of several persons of Quality a *Minuet* by Noverre and Mrs Palmer.
ENTERTAINMENT. A New Interlude, call'd the *Farmer's Return from London*. Farmer – Garrick; Farmer's Wife – Mrs Bradshaw.
COMMENT. Benefit for Mrs Pritchard. Part of Pit laid into Boxes.

THE JEALOUS WIFE. Oakly – Ross; Major Oakly – Shuter; Charles – Clarke; Lord Trinket – Dyer; Sir Harry Beagle – Bennet; Capt. O'Cutter – Barrington; Russet – Dunstall; Paris – Holtom; Tom – R. Smith; Harriet – Mrs Lessingham; Lady Freelove – Mrs Vincent; Mrs Oakly – Mrs Ward. Also FLORIZEL AND PERDITA. Florizel (with new songs in character) – Mattocks; Autolicus (with songs in character) – Shuter; King – Hull; Shepherd - Gibson; Perdita (with new songs in character) – Miss Brent. The Music composed by Dr Arne, with a *Dance* incident to the Pastoral by Granier, Mrs Granier, &c.   CG
DANCING. *The Pleasures of Spring*, as 12 Feb.
COMMENT. Benefit for Ross. Mainpiece: Never acted there. Afterpiece: Not acted this season. No Building on Stage. Tickets and Places to be had of Mr Ross in the Little Piazza, Covent Garden; and of Mr Sarjant, at the Stage Door.

FIGURE 1

(Reproduced by permission of Southern Illinois University Press from Volume II, page 923 of *The London Stage, 1660–1800, Part 4: 1747–1776*, edited by George Winchester Stone, Jr.)

well," I would say, "Sometimes an actor is delimited by a comma before and after." "Couldn't that delimit a role too? Can't roles come in a series?" I was never sure. Will on his part hated to write a program if he thought there were going to be any exceptions whatsoever to an item's standard delimiters. I would always lose this debate unless I could say that I had checked every entry in *The London Stage* and knew that such and such was always thus and so. I never reached that strategic height.

The problem, as I dimly understood then, and now do fairly well understand, was absolutely fundamental. We were starting an attempt to state precisely the form in which the text would be presented to the computer. Although we worked out something experimental for the MT/ST girls in a week, it was to take nearly six months to arrive at a firm version of the Specs. We would eventually produce eight editions. The last version, I hesitate to call it final because even the version of the text that now resides on magnetic tape can still be changed, was eleven typed pages long. The Specs were so crucial that a slight change in them shook the whole fabric of our enterprise as a constitutional amendment affects the whole pattern of life in a country.

I have said that a computer can "read" in the sense that it can tell whether a known word is the same as or different from an unknown word and that depending on whether the comparison succeeds or fails it can perform one action or another. The function of the Specs was to make sure that the computer could identify the various classes of things it contained and which it was our mission to make automatically accessible—such classes of things as titles, actors, and roles.

Most lists keep things in a form that helps us to tell what they are. Telephone books give the name first, the house number (if any) second, the street third, and the phone number last. Bibliographies and dictionaries also observe a strict order. And so, too, *The London Stage*, I insisted. Let the computer analyze the structure.

"Too much variation," Will explained. A computer can't tolerate as much ambiguity as a human. A human understands the language in which the list is written. He can tell from experience with names and addresses where in a phone book a name stops and an address begins because he recognizes the difference between a namelike and an addresslike thing. "Schultz" is probably a name and "Maple" is probably a street. A computer might be programmed to take advantage of such probabilities, but the program would have to be more complex than most computers could manage, containing large dictionaries of namelike and streetlike words, and allowing for the fact that a name need not be followed by initials, that a house may not have a number, that there are dozens of words for "street."

The human being uses an immense store of words to resolve ambiguities. Without understanding English how can a machine know that "Presbyterian Church" as it might appear in a telephone book is not a man with the first name "Church" and the last name "Presbyterian"? It is much easier to delimit the parts of every name by special symbols than to teach a computer to recognize "Presbyterian Church" as an exception to the last-name-first rule. Judicious delimiting can save an immense amount of programming.

On the other hand, a reasonable amount of programming can save a great deal of delimiting. Computer time, despite John Bachhuber's doubts, was free, like the library, to faculty engaged in research. We could work the computer more to work typists less. When a text is to be entered on a keyboard device every delimiter is another arbitrary and meaningless sign for the typist or keypunch operator to get wrong and which by distracting her can cause her to get other things wrong. Our task, I maintained, was to present the text well enough to enable the computer to find the place where any category of information resided with a minimum amount of meddling interference.

I saw, however, that the categories must be clearly delimited and follow each other in an undeviating order. To find, for example, every actor in an afterpiece the computer would first have to be able to identify the unit of text pertaining to events at one theatre on one day. Having done so it would have to identify the first play title and cast list, because it would have to skip those, and then it would have to recognize the second play title and cast list as an afterpiece section. Finally, having located the cast list it would have to be able to recognize which items were actors and which were roles.

Metaphorically, an actor in *The London Stage* is like a man living in a house which is his role, on a street, in a section of town. For example, in the section of text shown on our sample page (Figure 1) if you go down Calendar Highway to the Avenue Saturday the 20th, past the street called Drury Lane to the place called Covent Garden and take the first road you come to, called Jealous Wife Road, and if you go to the fourth house on this road, it is called Lord Trinket and in it lives Dyer. It would be lovely if every play road were designed like Jealous Wife Road, but as the page shows, many Play Roads have vacant entries that simply refer us to earlier casts. They have only signposts telling us to go back to a previous turning if we want to find the people living in their houses. They have been too lazy to move though they have sent word where they may be reached.

The city of *The London Stage* is not constructed like any city we ever saw before, being strung out endlessly on one long Calendar Highway. But we sense that we can map this city, that its streets, roads, and houses repeat in predictable ways, and that we can therefore give directions for finding each feature of the terrain. An actor, for example, always resides in a road off a street, off an avenue, off a highway. These thoroughfares must either follow each other in the same order always, so that we know that we always turn from an avenue to a street to a road or, if they don't come in the proper order, they must be labeled for what they are. As Will said, items must be concatenated in a rigid syntax or they must be tagged, and all fields must be clearly delimited.

Throughout these discussions I kept harping on the theme of "follow copy," and Will hammered away on the question of delimiters. As we talked, names began to emerge. Just as Adam learned about his universe by naming the animals we learned about ours by naming our basic units of text. The reader may identify the species for himself on our sample page. Everything at a theatre on a date came to be known as a "performance entry" (performance entries are signalled by the date and theatre notations in the margin; DL = Drury Lane, CG = Covent Garden). The date and theatre preceding the entry we would call the "header." A performance entry began with a "play," or to distinguish it from a second play, a "mainpiece" (the titles of the mainpieces jut out into the left margin). A play had a "title" which was usually followed by a "cast list" (*The Jealous Wife*, near the bottom, has a typical cast list). A cast list consisted of "roles" and "actors." All the part having to do with one play was a "section." Besides "play sections" there might be "afterpiece sections," introduced by the word "Also" (*Florizel and Perdita*, following *The Jealous Wife*, is an afterpiece). There were also "dancing sections," "singing sections" and "music sections" (*The Mistake* has dancing, *Tancred* has singing, and *Samson* has music).

In making these observations we were simply recognizing divisions, relations, and subordinations already well shown forth by the excellent typography of the Brüder Rosenbaum, as the reader can see from my sample page. But the structure brought out by typography was on closer inspection imperfect. Will identified in addition to "structured text" a more bothersome variety called "free text." By structured text he meant sections comprising the basic components of a performance arranged in a uniform order uniformly punctuated. Free text was composed randomly of unnameable units. This phenomenon troubled us sorely in the early days by spoiling the uniformity of structured text—as do the asides and parentheses in the cast list of the afterpiece *Florizel and Perdita* and the sentence at the end of that cast list that runs on incontinently about music and dancing and composers, having no business among actors and roles.

One day Will solved this problem with a resounding new name. "What are we going to do about all this 'extraneous text?' " he said. From then on "extraneous text" was our name for anything non-structured. I bridled a bit at the word, because nothing in *The London Stage* was truly extraneous, but it stuck. "I won't let you throw that text away," I said. "Can't we put it in brackets or something so it can be ignored for the time being but kept in the text for future processing by another method?" Thus extraneous text became a vacant lot full of weeds on a road of role houses, but delimited by "no trespassing" signs.

With this matter somewhat uneasily settled, we went on to describe more accurately the structure of structured text. A cast list in a play and afterpiece section always followed a title and it consisted of "cast groups." Cast groups had several forms but consisted mostly of a role-actor pair or a role with several actors (as in "Officers — Scrase, Castle, &c" in *Tancred*) or possibly just a role or just an actor, when who played what was not known, though the who or what was.

Singing and dancing were a bit recalcitrant at first. Notice that on the 20th at Drury Lane, we have, after bracketing the extraneous text, dancing which consists of "A Minuet by Noverre and Mrs Palmer." For a while, because the text used a preposition and a coordinating conjunction, we thought we had discovered a new species, but in truth it was the same old house and lodger situation as before. "Syntactic role and syntactic actors," said Will. "Same as a role with two actors. Minuet is a syntactic role." It now dawned on me forcibly what Richard Golden had meant when he urged "syntactic analysis" on me. I was as delighted as Molière's Bourgeois Gentilhomme had been to discover that he had been speaking prose all his life. I had been doing syntactic analysis for two weeks! It really wasn't much different from diagramming sentences, except that English is many degrees more general in application, as a noun is many degrees more general than an actor. Thus in dancing sections a dancer was a syntactic actor and his dance a syntactic role. In singing sections the singer was a syntactic actor and his song a syntactic role. In music sections, wonder of wonders, the musician could be construed as an actor, his instrument as a syntactic role, and the piece as a syntactic title. This meant that by designing programs to fit a basic play-role-actor syntax, Will would simultaneously deal with singing, dancing, and music.

Another nasty situation was created by the great number of references to earlier casts which had already come up at the Carbondale meeting. Only by this device could the editors prevent the work from becoming 110 volumes instead of eleven. One advantage of using the computer was that all these empty cast lists could be automatically filled with their proper tenants. Adopting *The London Stage*'s official term, we called these forwarding addresses (more properly backwarding addresses) "ladder references." There were simple and complex ladder references: simple

when in the form "As 18 Jan.," complex when in the form
"As 11 Dec., but King Henry – Gibson." These revisions
of the cast brought forward, Will said one day, were "ladder updates," and so "ladder updates" they became. Singing and dancing contained a species not found in other sections which we called "time notations." At Covent Garden
on the 18th we are informed by the Roman numeral three
that dancing took place in, before, or after Act III of *Henry
IV* and at Drury Lane on the 20th there was some dancing
at the "End of Play." These time notations, we decided,
could not be ignored as extraneous, and we would have to
take measures to present them to the computer unambigu-
ously.

One more class of text arose from our being commissioned by the Southern Illinois Press to supply a comprehensive index. We were confident of being able to
extract all names and titles in the structured text automatically. But cruder methods would be required for extraneous text. Comments and other parenthetical elements
contained a great many names and titles that must be
captured for the Southern Illinois Press index. "Index entries," as we called them, would have to be delimited and
if possible tagged to denote the kind of name or title they
were, whether play, song, role, manager, orange-girl, street,
dog, or horse. Most index entries were to be found in the
comments, but other sections also contained them. At
Drury Lane on the 17th *New Serenata* and "Dr Arne"
would be delimited as index entries. And at Covent Garden
on the same day "their Majesties" is an index entry.

Our study of *London Stage* syntax, while it turned up
a few nasty exceptions, also divulged a most welcome
amount of uniformity. The editors and Vernon had established sound syntactical rules and held to them. Hence I
received with some consternation Will's declaration one
day that each section—play, afterpiece, singing, dancing, or

music—must be preceded by a red MT/ST code letter
and followed by a slash and that each performance entry
must end with a slash followed by an asterisk. I refused to
believe that Will really needed these special marks. Plays,
I pointed out, always came first in an entry. Afterpieces
when present always came second and were preceded by
the word "Also." Other sections were always headed by
words in capital letters which clearly distinguished them as
section headings. Will wanted to put in exclusively non-
textual indicators. "Also," he noted, could appear anywhere. How were we to describe to the computer which
"Also"s were false, and how much time was this programming worth? Section headings like "SINGING" and
"DANCING" would also be a bother. Why not simply
use a red *s* or a red *d* to denote singing and dancing sections? It would shorten the typists' work. Up against this
logic, I conceded that abbreviated section codes like this,
as long as they mnemonically identified the sections they
preceded, would indeed be more efficient than following
copy and have little if any nuisance value.

I continued to resist his slash at the end of each section, however. The red letter was there already. Why did
he need double warning of the beginning of a new section
and the end of an old? After working with data using the
slashes for a few days, Will conceded this pont. Thus a
performance entry came to be delimited by an asterisk and
each section of it by a red initial indicating the content.
Then the asterisks went, too, with the realization that every
performance entry began with a red *p* for play, a sufficient
announcement that a new theatrical avenue was being ex-
plored.

At first, it looked to Will as if there were no way to
tell where a play title ended and a cast list began. Not
until I guaranteed that I would cause a period plus two
spaces to mark the end of every title would he drop the red

r that he had fixed on to announce the end of a title and the beginning of a cast list. I thought we could depend on any experienced typist to put two spaces after any complete unit of text ending in a period, especially considering that *The London Stage* also followed this convention. The danger of course was that items themselves might contain abbreviations followed by periods. I swore that convention would decree one space after a period following an abbreviation when any titles like St. Joan or initials like C. Bullock occurred.

Having seen the wisdom of compressing section headings I made no objection to Will's proposal for capturing the date and theatre information by simply stating it consistently in a given order after the red *p* announcing a new performance entry. We could follow the practice of *The London Stage* itself taking note of the day, month, or year only when it changed. The computer could remember the unchanging part of the date. As long as the date always appeared in year-month-day order when more than one element was given, one space between each element was all the delimiting required. Following the date came the theatre abbreviation ready-made by the editors of *The London Stage* and after that, preceded by one space, came the title of the mainpiece. The days of the week could be discarded, Will said; they could easily be restored by a well-known formula if anyone wanted to know.

The brilliant simplicity with which Will's date-theatre header coped with several important facts in a clear, simple, and compact form so naturally derived from the conventions of the text as to seem inevitable and so reasonable as to require no thought from the typist was to me a perfect example of how working with computers sharpens one's logical capacity. My previous training had given me a less rational approach. A tiny matter that produced a large disagreement between Will and me marvelously illustrates the difference between us. When I wrote up the Specs for the typists, I said "Put one space after each item of a date-theatre unit." When Will checked the draft, he insisted that I say, "Put at least one space after each item," because two or several would not cause any harm, the way he would program it. I objected that creating options and alternatives would only worry the typists. He refused to approve an untruth. The reason for this and many similar disagreements, as I look back on it, was that we approached the Specs from opposite positions. He wished simply to describe what his program would and would not accept. I wanted to state in the fewest and simplest words rules by which acceptable data could be prepared. I could not abide latitude that created needless choices for the typist. Will's approach was descriptive like that of some grammarians, and mine was prescriptive like that of other grammarians and perhaps for the same reasons. Will regarded the machine and I regarded the human provider of the machine.

We had decided to postpone programming for ladder references until we had solved the fundamental question of retrieving data in its essential form. It looked to Will as though the most common kind of ladder update, "As 24 Sept. 1761, but Tancred – Garrick," could be interpreted by the computer without any extra delimiters; it would appear in a cast group "field" but it could easily be distinguished from a cast group by the presence of the date and the words "As" and "but." Some ladder references, however, in which informal language had been used, as in "As 14 Nov., but Mrs Mills now joins the Furies and Mrs Wills is now a Harpy," would have to be rewritten in a stricter syntax of our own devising.

Our strategy was to allow the natural syntax of *The London Stage* as far as possible to delimit items in structured text. But there were times when most distressingly the text had more than one way of expressing a single phenomenon.

It was easier to normalize the text than to program for exceptions. The most frequent deviation from standard syntax was the use of the word "by" instead of a hyphen to indicate a syntactical actor and the use of the word "and" instead of a comma to denote the last member of a series of syntactical actors or roles. "Minuet by Noverre and Mrs Palmer" is an example of this deviant syntax. There was nothing for it but to betray my oath to follow copy and ask the typists to recognize this commonest form of "bad grammar" and correct it. I regretted that I would be making their job very sensibly harder.

But it would be impossible for anyone not especially trained to locate the names and titles in extraneous text that were destined to become index entries. Nevertheless, if the text was to be at all computable, these index entries would have to be delimited. The solution forced on us was for me to mark them before typing and have the typist put in the delimiters when she saw the marks. Nor could the typists be expected to isolate and delimit many segments of extraneous text not already set off naturally by brackets or parentheses in the source. Since the text itself used the natural delimiters we had to find something else for text we found still to be extraneous, like "By Particular Desire of several persons of Quality" introducing the "Minuet by Noverre and Mrs Palmer" on the 20th at Drury Lane. We decided to use red brackets even though on the MT/ST keyboard it took two shifts to produce an opening bracket, one for upper case and one to make it red. Will had a violent prejudice against unnecessary key strokes; data services charge by the keystroke. So he persuaded me that because real brackets occurred less in the text than our artificial inserted brackets would, the real brackets should be in red and the inserted ones should be the common garden variety. We thus gave the typist another chore: instead of following copy, when the text uses black

1) performance header: '*pdd mm yy tttt play. '

2.1) play section: '*play. cast list. '

2.2) cast list section: '*xcast list. '

2.21) cast list: 'cast group; cast group; cast group. '

2.211) cast group: 'part-performer; '
                  'part-performer, performer; '
                  'performer, performer; '
                  'part, part-performer; '
                  'part, part-; '
                  '"as" reference'
                  '"as" reference, update'
                  '"see" reference'
                  '"see" reference, update'

2.212) time: 'time: cast group; '

2.3) comment section: '*cextraneous text index-item extraneous text'

2.31) index-item: '$name='
               '+title='

3) extraneous text: '(extraneous text)'
                    '[extraneous text]'
                    '[extraneous text%'
                    '*cextraneous text*x'

Notes. Spacing is an element of syntax. Single quotation marks enclose items of syntax but are not part of syntax. Numbers indicate degree of subordination.

1) '*' precedes section signal. 'p' indicates performance entry. 'd' is number of day, 'm' is number of month, 'y' is number of year, and 't' is a letter of the London Stage abbreviation of the theatre.

2.1) 'x' is a letter signifying the kind of section that follows (play, song, dance, music, etc.). It also conveys the structure of the section.

2.21) A series of cast groups may be as long as necessary.

2.211) A series of parts or performers may be as long as necessary. Any combination of cast groups in any order is allowed, except that only one type of reference is allowed in a play section and it must come first in the cast list.

3) Extraneous text may precede or follow any item in a performance entry. It is a character string of indeterminate length. Extraneous text of any sort may contain index items.

FIGURE 2

brackets, convert them to red. When brackets are editorially inserted (probably with a red pencil) make them black.

Will's invention of extraneous text proved to be more useful than we ever had expected it would be. By judicious use of the concept we could set aside knotty problems for later treatment while he forged ahead on basic programming. We could simply delimit nasty bits of text as temporarily extraneous. Eventually in the process of proofreading our magnetic tape we would write these bypassed sections in syntax acceptable to our programs.

Over many months of trial and error and toil and trouble which I cannot begin to convey here, Will and I began to sense the ideal and true Platonic form of *The London Stage*, the essential map of actors in their role houses on the roads of the streets of the avenues of that great city. We developed a standard syntax that could express nearly everything and that with a minimum amount of editing could express the particle that remained. The underlying structure, as it turned out, was simple. Even though it took ten pages to explain our Specs to the MT/ ST typists, their final state can be summarized for an initiate on one page. Since anyone who has come this far is an initiate I show forth the essence of *The London Stage* under the rubric of Figure 2. Here, shorn of all extraneous dross and all transitory variation, worked out slowly by dialectic, is the FORM of *The London Stage, 1660–1800*.

CHAPTER IV

OF
IMPLEMENTATION

*The Author interfaces an MT/ST Pool. He explores
Route 128, observes Bolt, Beranek and Newman, Digital
Equipment Company & Viatron. He shops in the Yellow
Pages of Boston & encounters John Chan. Will delivers
some printouts. How Will's programs work, demonstrated
with Flowcharts. How Flowcharts work. The second
Advisory Board Meeting, with a digression on Indexing.
The Author enquires about Optical Scanning & Cathode
Ray Terminals, meets the Grand Old Man of Offshore
Keypunching, deduces an Ideal Input Device, & grades
real ones. He hunts down a compatible Character Set.
Superfluity of Funds. Experiments with Optical Scanning.
His search for John Chan & conversations with David
Shiu. He discovers ICI.*

The MT/ST's at the Institute of Paper Chemistry
responded well to the challenge of *The London
Stage*. We met Byron Grow, manager of the MT/ST
pool, Quita, his chief of staff, and Betty and Mary early
one morning in late October in a seminar room. There I
began enthusiastically to illustrate on the blackboard how it

was we wanted this text to be typed. It was fortunate that these girls had had some experience with computer input, because although they were mystified by what I told them they were not dismayed. They were used to being mystified. It didn't help much that Will and I began revising the Specs in the middle of the session. I believe that Quita asked, after the session had been going for about an hour, why we didn't do it the way they did the chemistry abstracts. I suggested that perhaps if one of the girls simply started typing some of our data, we might be able to ex-plain better when we saw what they did.

With Will and me looking over her shoulder and criticizing, Mary soon produced several pages of text. Byron put her MT/ST tape on the Digidata converting machine to make a computer tape out of it, and Will rushed off to the computer to see what he had. Next day when he randomly appeared as usual at my office rubbing his eyes, the first thing I wanted to know was how the MT/ST output looked. "Oh yes, I wanted to tell you about that. We're getting a lot of garbage mixed in with the data." Apparently the Digidata was acting up. Will eventually tried to avoid garbage by having Mary put a delimiter at the end of every MT/ST page, but the Digidata con-tinued off and on to cause trouble.

The MT/ST girls were a very quiet group. Except for occasional garbage and our tendency to change the Specs from day to day as programming suggested different forms of input, everything seemed to be going well.

There was a possibility that the MT/ST might be a good device for editing our text after conversion. This would most certainly be necessary to correct non-syntacti-cal passages, and it seemed impossible that any conversion process could be error free. Perhaps the MT/ST's tape-editing system was the answer to our prayers. But in order to use it we would either have to find a reverse Digidata machine for converting computer tape back to MT/ST tape or keep all our MT/ST tapes and edit and reconvert them when we wanted to improve our computer version. One simple calculation, however, quashed the latter possibility. An MT/ST tape could hold 23,000 characters; *The London Stage* contained 21,000,000 characters, ergo roughly 1000 MT/ST tapes; one MT/ST tape cost $20, 1000 tapes $20,000. But there must be a way to convert computer tape to MT/ST tape.

In Mary's hands the MT/ST worked fine as an editing device. She would search to the paragraph containing the mistake, transferring all the text to a new tape as she went. Then she would cause the machine to type up to the word or sentence to be revised, stop the old tape, put the revision on the new tape and finish copying the good part of the old tape. To accomplish this editing process she manipulated keys for insert and delete, for transfer to the lefthand and to the righthand tape, for recording on the left and on the right, and for playing the left and right tape. She made it look very easy. One weekend I decided I would try to revise the Specs myself which were kept on an MT/ST tape for Mary to revise. I spent six hours one afternoon attempting to fix four short passages and finished the day with a worse version of the Specs than I had started with. My trouble was a simple inability to do the right thing at the right time. I would transfer when I should record, play when I should transfer, lose my place on the new tape, forget where I was on the old tape, create new errors by recording on top of good text. Every time I failed I had to start at the beginning of the old tape and type automatically to the place where I'd bungled. I thought there must be easier ways to do this.

The girls had been typing our data during slack times for about a month and a half and had converted about thirty pages of text, when one morning I received the following letter from Byron:

Ben and Will:

For the time being, we will have to put you on a schedule in order to get our own work done.

If you have any recording to do, bring it in at 3:00 and leave it with instructions to the typist. Come back and pick it up just before 5:00. Please DO NOT stand by typist while she is doing the work as she is getting quite upset over this. (I don't want to lose a typist.) Also, I understand that they are getting upset as you will not follow (or try) their suggestions as far as recording goes. When we first discussed this, you were quite willing to have the typist tell you how to record this so that there would be some sequence of operation. Right now they are ready to chuck the whole thing.

Byron

This reaction came as a total surprise to us. I never did find out what specific misdeeds Byron referred to. Apparently our attempts to show the typist what we wanted as she typed, our frequent alterations of the Specs, and our ideas about how to get around the garbage, even the fact that any garbage had fallen on the tapes at all, were construed as negative criticism of the MT/ST pool. In an attempt to understand I began with the fact that the girls were offended at our not following their suggestions for data entry. Remembering Quita's remark about doing it the same way as chemistry abstracts I thought I could see how our behavior might look to the girls in the pool. Perhaps they had begun to think after years of typing chemistry abstracts that the rules they followed were rules for the computer. One says, incorrectly, time and again, "If you don't do it this way, the computer will reject it." To people who had mastered the computer as a chemistry abstract machine our heedless *London Stage* antics must have seemed foolhardy and pigheaded in the extreme. We told Byron we were sorry and we never entered the MT/ST room again but used him always as our intermediary. Apparently everything was all right after that. A few days later we were exchanging smiles in the snack bar and waves in the parking lot.

We would not know, at any rate, whether the MT/ST was the best way to enter our data without investigating other alternatives. I was teaching a single Tuesday-Thursday-Saturday class, and that meant that only a Saturday morning class stood in the way of having Thanksgiving weekend free. I decided to teach a double class on Tuesday morning, then fly to Boston to spend Thanksgiving with my parents and to seek counsel in that hub of the computing universe.

Certain accidents of residence helped me to get acquainted. My parents lived in Winchester, only a few miles from the famous electronic and computing brain belt that rings Boston on Route 128. Dick Best, who had something to do with Digital Equipment Company, had summered for sixteen years in the camp (cottage) next to ours in New Hampshire. And in Winchester, Leo Beranek, of the think tank named Bolt, Beranek and Newman, lived two houses up the hill from my parents.

The Beraneks had been most hospitable to us during our stay in my parents' house the previous summer. It was Leo Beranek, in fact, who during that summer of information retrieval about informations retrieval had first given me an inside glimpse of the astonishing cultural blend that characterizes scientific and technological enterprise around Boston: MIT, Harvard, Radcliffe, Paul Tillich, Noam

Chomsky, Norbert Wiener, James Bryant Conant, Serge Koussevitsky, Thoreau, Senator Saltonstall, the Dartmouth Outing Club, Los Alamos, the Boston & Maine Railroad, the *Mayflower*, Emily Dickinson, Benjamin Franklin, Joan Baez, the VW bus, the sailing canoe, A. D. Little, and Howard Johnson's are a few of the things that go into the mixture.

One afternoon Leo had arranged for me to visit the people at his firm who it seemed were most likely to be able to help me. BB & N (short for Bolt, Beranek and New-man) do just about any kind of research. They designed and adjusted acoustics for the Lincoln Center, figured out what colors are best for painting hospital rooms and explained to the Massachusetts Transport Authority that their subway trains screech on curves because they don't use two-piece axles that allow the outside wheel to go faster than the inside, and designed and implemented the first commercial time-sharing telephone-a-computer service (Telcomp). This renowned research organization occupies a group of old garages north of Cambridge not far from the Alewife Brook Parkway, where the Dewey and Almy Chemical Corporation used to be and the rail-road yards spread desolation and the storage tanks abound. The main entrance faces the street, at the top of a three-foot-wide cement staircase with an iron pipe railing. Inside, the reception room is neatly furnished but there is no decor anywhere in sight. The receptionist, who is simply a nice lady, sits behind a window with a hole in it, as in a factory, and rings Mr. Beranek for you.

Aside from these industrial suggestions, visiting BB & N was like visiting an academic institution except that most of the people seemed more like faculty than students. I circulated first among some of the senior faculty and then among some of the junior programmers and analysts who were dealing with problems much like mine. The atmosphere was intellectual rather than businesslike. I asked two of the younger fellows, the second having drifted in to join my conversation with the first for no apparent reason, why they were interested in talking to me. "We always enjoy talking to people with similar applications. It helps us keep up in our specialties." I was too much of a neophyte at this time to profit as much from this visit as I might have, but I did take home some information about routines for searching a large data base, and a copy of their excellent step by step instructions for using Telcomp. It was there I learned for the first time that the computers of different manufacturers used different internal codes for numbers and letters: old IBM machines used Binary Coded Decimal (BCD); new IBM machines used Extended Binary Coded Decimal Interchange Code (EBCDIC —pronounced "Ibb'seedick"); and other machines used the American Standard Code for Information Interchange (ASCII—pronounced "Asky"). Looking back, I realize that one of the most remarkable things about the people at BB & N was that, unlike most computer people I have met, they acted as if a *London Stage* Information Bank was a perfectly natural human activity.

It was not until they showed me BB & N's computer that I realized that the famous and pervasive PDP (Programmed Data Processor) series of computers, of which the PDP/8 was most common, were made by Digital Equipment Company. I had known that our summer neighbor Dick Best worked for Digital something or other but I hadn't known that Digital made the PDP series until I actually saw the labels on BB & N's computer. Sometime before Thanksgiving, therefore, I called up Dick Best to see if he thought a visit to his factory in Maynard would be appropriate. I wanted to discuss converting Monotype tape, alternatives to the MT/ST, and Lawrence's plans for improving its computer facility. Dick did think DEC (pronounced "deck") could help on all three fronts; we arranged to meet at the Maynard factory at 10:00 a.m. on the Wednesday before Thanksgiving.

Maynard is still rural enough to remind one that Thoreau once roamed its woods. Like many New England towns it has a dam in its river just above the center and a jumble of old red brick mills mellowing toward purple beneath the dam. DEC apparently occupied all the mill buildings in Maynard center, and they were all connected by abutment at some angle or another or by covered bridges, and the river got through them somehow.

The main entrance from the visitors' disintegrating asphalt parking lot was a wooden footbridge across a gully into an upper floor of one of the factory buildings. One entered a fairly large, brightly lighted, unadorned, carpet-less section of a loft with a counter and door at the far end. At the counter a motherly person helped one write down one's business on a card and asked one to take a seat in a row of about seven chairs down the middle of the room. There were a few dog-eared magazines to look at. It was impossible to deduce the principle of their selection or the series of accidents by which they had arrived here. *Colorado Municipalities, Cat-Lover's Digest, Psychology Today.*

In about five minutes a secretary arrived whose mission was to take me to Mr. Best. Down echoing cement staircases, over covered bridges, through dark brick tunnels, up narrow wooden stairs, through large empty rooms we went to an immense, teeming single room with a twelve-foot ceiling, containing maybe fifty or one hundred offices. She took me to where in one of these offices—to me indis-tinguishable from any others in the building—I found Dick Best drawing some electronic diagrams on a blackboard.

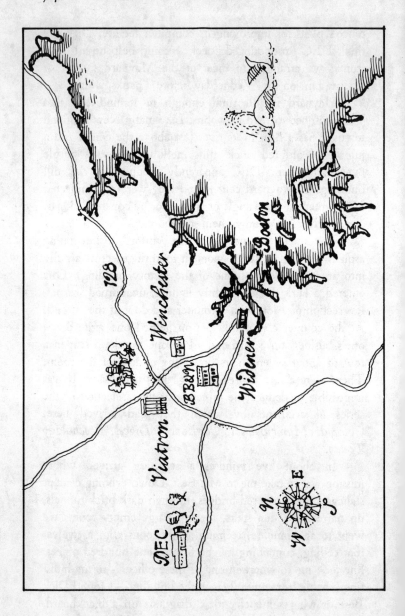

These offices had been set up in a large loft of the factory on an acre of original splintery old fir floor. They consisted of plywood partitions just about head high, strung up on a vast network of two-by-fours. There were openings to go in and out of the resultant cubicles but no doors. The whole array looked as if it might have been assembled in four days, one day for the two-by-fours, one day for the telephones and electricity, one day for plywood, and one day for paint. Decoration was sparse and consisted of posters; I remember mainly some handsome DEC posters and some ski posters. Our offices at Lawrence, of average academic dowdiness, seemed sumptuous compared to this barn full of stalls.

After talking to me for a while to see what I was up to and what would be the best way for me to spend my time, Dick very kindly showed me various points of interest. I saw PDP/8's trouble-shooting each other. I saw a PDP/8 whose duty was composing and editing company publications. I saw DEC's amazing system for photographing, developing, etching, plating, and reproducing printed circuits. I saw a vast empty loft. "We've run out of labor in the Maynard area," Dick explained. "We've had to build a new factory in Marlboro." I saw water coolers and Coke machines and grey paint and whitewash and splintery old floors and timbered roofs with joists uncovered and fluorescent lights hanging down. Nowhere a carpet. Not even linoleum. Nowhere a drape. Nowhere cement, glass, steel, and chromium plate.

After our tour, Dick took me to some marketing people who'd done some research on alternatives to the MT/ST. I expected more sumptuous digs for the public interface of the company, but we stood on the same splintery footing as in Dick's office. In the course of our conversations, I discovered that my summer neighbor was no less than DEC's chief engineer and that he wore the company's identification badge number 20. "But his office is the same as everyone else's," I remarked. "Not exactly," they replied, "He has a table and a bigger blackboard and about ten extra square feet." Also I remembered he had a window, a luxury denied the masses in the central region. Nobody appeared to have a secretary, but in several clearings among the offices were groups of typist-reception-ist-secretary types, ministering, possibly discriminately, in these capacities to the offices.

My talks at DEC were similar to those at BB & N. The people there had the same purely academic interest in the *London Stage* Information Bank's problems. Everyone except Dick seemed to be in his twenties or early thirties. They dropped into each other's offices to talk shop, they drew on each other's blotters and blackboards, accessed the company's computer from each other's teletypes. Their PDP/8's were much involved in scientific research, and they were interested in developing their market for com-puter typesetting and for time-sharing computers in schools and colleges. Although they competed with IBM, their origins and inclinations seemed to be more academic than commercial.

It was decided that I would have lunch with one of the marketing consultants. He borrowed a friend's car and took me to a restaurant that would have been Howard Johnson's if there'd been one in Maynard. We had no drinks and ate frugally while we discussed my problems and computers in general. He was interested in the *London Stage* Information Bank simply as another form of computer application. One probably could not have told from our discussion that his job was selling computers. After lunch we visited an engineer in the applications section of the company—a silky-voiced young Indian from India having that typical delicate accent that seems to caress English rather than distort it—to talk about Monotype conversion. He talked a good bit and drew block diagrams on his blotter, one block, naturally enough, always being a PDP/8 to convert Monotype codes to computer codes. For alternatives to the MT/ST the DEC people recommended a data entry device made by the Viatron Company, using a cathode ray tube (CRT) terminal as a data entry device. Dick Best thought it must be a good terminal because DEC made circuit boards for Viatron. An appointment with Viatron marketing was arranged for four that afternoon.

Viatron, they told me, was on Route 128 next to a big shopping center called the Burlington Mall (Sears Roebuck, Jordan Marsh, Filene's, Radio Shack). Having followed directions and sighted no Viatron, I assumed I had mistook the directions. Across the street from the Mall was a large industrial park full of small companies with names compounded out of syllables like "tronic," "tech," "elec," "compu," "matic," "data," "digi," "mation," "info," "auto," "proto," "photo," "micro," "macro," and so forth. I drove open-mouthed around them but there was no "Viatron" among the syllables.

At a filling station they told me to look in some buildings behind a supermarket up the road. I found a building containing three stores which were being used as small factories or small warehouses. On the back door of one was written "Viatron." I rang the bell and banged on the door. Nobody was there. Through an open door in the next unit I saw some men who were boxing electronic devices. "I'm trying to find Viatron," I called. "Lots of people are trying to find Viatron," they called back, laughing. They had no further suggestions.

At a drugstore in the supermarket complex I was told I couldn't possibly miss Viatron. "One mile further north, turn left, third building on the left." By now it was past four, and I began to think that I was doing Route 128's version of the search for the left-handed monkey wrench. But I charged up to the intersection, turned left, soon found myself in front of a large new glass, steel, and concrete building that looked like the temple of Karnak in the middle of a carefully cultured lawn, with the letters "VIATRON" emblazoned on it in a size you could not miss. The reception hall had a ceiling three stories high, and I have to say it was window-to-window carpeted because there was so much more window than wall.

At the foot of an elegant staircase sat a blonde at an impressive facility consisting of a desk, a switchboard, a computer terminal, and a typewriter. She informed me that I really wanted Viatron's Marketing Division. This I would find next to the Burlington Mall. It resided in a large set of office buildings of which they occupied a suite in building A. I knew exactly where she meant. While she called to tell them I was on my way I screeched over to the Burlington Mall as in a spy thriller, and soon found myself in a cosy plush reception room explaining my business to another blonde.

Soon a marketing consultant appeared and took me into an office full of electronic equipment, manned by an older blonde. Here I saw my first text-entering and text-editing cathode ray tube computer terminal in action. It had a small TV screen that displayed four lines of text. From its keyboard you could correct any part of it. When you were satisfied, the text could be sent to a computer. In the practiced hands of its mistress, it performed sends, receives, inserts, deletes, and changes perfectly. But though I liked its tricks, it had two great drawbacks from the point of view of the *London Stage* Information Bank. It would not display as much as one typical *London Stage* entry at a time; and it did not have a full upper and lower case character set. Apparently it had been conceived of as a keypunch replacement: It used the keypunch's limited character set and behaved as if it displayed four IBM cards at a time. It was cheaper and better than a keypunch but not as good as it could be for handling text.

I was one of the last people to see Viatron alive. A few months later its bankruptcy became the scandal of the computer trade. Viatron, the story went, had been a tremendous gamble that failed. The original concept was simple, to produce the most efficient data entry system at the lowest cost that modern technology could enable. Losses would be phenomenal at first because the price would have to be ridiculously low to drive out the perennial keypunch. This daring idea at first brought in massive financial backing. By the time I appeared on the stage, production was under way and a major advertising campaign using five-page foldouts in the back of the principal computing journals was in progress. But salesmanship was not enough. People began to suspect that Viatron was a big hot air balloon and it burst. Comparing DEC and Viatron, I concluded that industrial substance varies inversely with appearance. Apparently some of Benjamin Franklin's philosophy still prevailed in Boston's brain belt. It was he who observed that "the sound of your hammer in your shop at five in the morning or eight at night" is the best way to gain credit in the world.

Friday morning after Thanksgiving I had another appointment at Viatron, this time to try out their terminal myself to see how it compared with the MT/ST. I discovered that it wasn't very easy to learn. But while I was waiting in the reception room for the sales representative to appear, my eye had fallen on a copy of *Electronic Engineer* announcing on its cover a review of computer display terminals. My heart beat faster as I leafed through several dozen pages describing scores of candidates for my editing job. Viatron was by no means the only applicant. As I departed, I paused to identify and write down the name and number of this journal for future reference. "Take it," said the marketing man and I did. Did I detect a note of despair in his voice?

I spent Friday afternoon shopping in Boston's Yellow Pages under the heading of data processing, which in that telephone book constituted a roll call of most of the major and minor computing companies in the U.S. With some amusement I discovered that DEC and Bolt, Beranek and Newman contented themselves with one line each of fine print, and while DEC and IBM allowed themselves bold-face, firms like Control Data, General Electric, RCA, and Honeywell, for whom disaster was always reported to be imminent, trumpeted their hard and soft wares in ostentatious boxes.

Having heard Curt Benster rave about "optical scanning" at the Purdue meeting, I had kept my ears open for news of it. Mechanical recognition of written or printed characters now had, after many years of people saying it couldn't be done, been done. It had even been suggested to me that a machine could read the pages of *The London Stage*. So I called the Boston office of the scanning firm known as REI (Recognition Equipment, Incorporated) and told the marketing representative who answered that I had 21,000,000 characters in eleven volumes that I wanted recognized. "The man you want to talk to," he said, "is Del Knowler at Corporation S in Dallas." "But what about REI?" I asked. "That's REI in Dallas. In Boston all we read is checks and that sort of thing."

I must confess I was very dubious about this reference. The man on the telephone had brushed me off as if I just called the wrong number. I had to get used to the fact that the United States was just like a big village to computer men, that to them long distance dollars were like local nickels and hopping on a plane was like hopping on a bus. Not having adjusted yet to this national village attitude I am ashamed to admit that it took me a month and a half to call all that distance to Del Knowler.

Instead of calling Dallas that afternoon, I browsed among the more than 75 companies whose terminals were listed in *Electronic Engineer*. One of the Boston companies, called Foto-Mem, supplied a terminal with "editing capabilities." This sounded promising, so I tried the number. I was in due course plugged into a telephone that replied, "John Chan here." I spelled that out to be sure, "C-H-A-N?" (resisting "Same as Charlie?"). I explained my text entry problem. "Ben," said John, "our Fotovision II is designed with such applications as yours in mind." He admitted, when pressed, making light of the matter, that upper and lower case were not "implemented at the present time." With editing, the terminal would cost $3495.

Electronic Engineer listed another terminal manufacturer in Woburn, the next town to the north of Winchester. Perhaps I could run over and take a look. The president of the company answered the phone. "We don't make any CRT's." "But *Electronic Engineer* . . ." "Oh, that was a year ago. I thought we told them to cancel that."

Honeywell, who had an office in Wellesley, was also listed as manufacturing a terminal. The man in marketing to whom they put me through said, "Oh yes, that would be peripherals." It turned out to be one of those calls where you explain your business and wait three to eleven minutes while the man or woman sees what he can find out and you repeat the process six or seven times until they discover they don't know who handles people like you and finally some-one warmly and cordially invites you to call again Mon-day.

Thus ended my first exploration of the brain belt. It was quitting time, and my thoughts turned to cold turkey, not on the drawing board but ready to serve, plattered and fully implemented.

When I returned to Appleton, December was upon us and Will and I had to have some results to show the Ad-visory Board at the Modern Language Association con-vention just after Christmas. Will had made good progress in programming by now, and there were many things we could now do with our growing sample of MT/ST text besides cull the garbage.

If Will's everyday logic might be said to have classical simplicity and his programming routines Baroque elegance, one might equally say that his early printouts were excellent examples of Gothic architecture. I shall never forget the first printout he brought me; it was output of the first version of a program that he called matter-of-factly SAVEDT, whose function was to display the MT/ST text in such a way that it would be easy to discover, locate, and fix errors: to save editing. One random evening hour, he brought a thick chunk of printout around to my house and we laid it out on the dining room table. "What is this?" I asked. "A printout." "I mean a printout of what?" "That stuff the MT/ST girls have been typing for us." There is a Vermont joke that has two fellows discussing some sheep on a distant hillside. "Looks as if Leverett has sheared his sheep," says one. " 'Pears so from this side," says the other. Will had the same healthy prejudice against asserting things you couldn't be sure of, not generated from any long experience of the uncertainties of farming but a lesson learned from watching the wreckage produced by computers fed with snap judgments about the nature of things.

The SAVEDT printout was what it was but, like many computer printouts I have known, was not typographically designed with its use in mind. In short, Will's first *London Stage* printout did not do justice to his virtuosity as a programmer. Text was chopped arbitrarily into blocks one MT/ST page long. Lines were numbered from one to the end of the block, thus giving no real clue to the absolute location of the line. Across the top and down the side were numbers, as in a graph, that would enable you, if you had a T-square, to find the exact co-ordinates of any letter in any line. Each passage of text was introduced by a legend, set off by a dozen asterisks: "LISTING REQUESTED OF INPUTBLOCK NO. 012, OUTPUT BLK NUMBER WILL BE 012. BLK 012 HAS A LENGTH OF 1498. REF CODE 012 OF MT/ST TAPE NO. 010." The right margin contained a column of phrases remarking "AT 0034, AT 0756, AT 1249." This gloss, it became apparent, gave the coordinates at which new sections began. Finally came the error messages, decorated by more asterisks: "BINDX [bad index entry] AT 03125; FUNP [funny page] AT 3329." This litany suggested the rubric of a medieval manuscript, with its "Explicit secunda pars eundem. Incipit tertia pars." Having spent the best years of my life looking at text I was used to finding things by the way they were arranged on the page—by indentations, spacing, punctuation, headings. I never could have thought of giving places in a text geometrical loci; if you want to show where a new section begins, why not just put a blank line in front of it and indent it?

Remembering Lewis Sawin's warning about results I urged Will to press on with programs that would pull names, titles, actors, and roles out of the computer tapes that Byron and the girls had made for us and list them alphabetically, to show the Advisory Board that we could in fact make an index with a computer. Accordingly, Will devoted himself to programs he called STRUCTUR, ITEMGET, and FORMAT. Meanwhile I pursued further the question of optical character recognition. I had recently read an article on the subject in *Computers and the Humanities,* a journal to which I had often turned for wisdom during the past few years. In it a gentleman named R. S. Morgan listed REI, Compuscan, and Scandata as manufacturers of machines that could read text. These three I instantly wrote, sending a Xeroxed page of *The London Stage* and a brief explanation of my input problem. Now I even believed enough in Del Knowler at Corporation S in Dallas to risk a letter to him.

In less than a week Edward Botsko of Dissly Systems Corporation, Easton, Pennsylvania, a firm I had not written, was on the phone: "Professor Schneider," he said, making no bones of the matter, "Our scanner can read your book." While I was adjusting to this astonishing information, he explained that Scandata had referred my letter to Dissly Systems because Dissly was a service bureau and they were not. He meant exactly what I thought he meant. Dissly could run the actual pages of *The London Stage* through their scanner and give me a magnetic tape of the text. What's more, they could insert codes for font changes and format features as they went. Since section headings in *The London Stage* did involve font changes, and date-theatre information in the margin was a prominent format feature, Dissly could not only read the book automatically, but they could automatically insert most of our red codes. They couldn't, however, find and mark our index entries or our extraneous text not already delimited by parentheses or brackets.

Ed was very reluctant to give me a figure for performing this job. He wanted to have some actual pages from the book for his systems people to study. The figure I finally forced out of him was, disappointingly, as high as Meade Data's for typing it all over again, but he left me the hope that if the quality of the print was high the cost would be lower. Counting on the flawless work of Brüder Rosenbaum to accomplish a drastic reduction I proposed that Edward come to New York and discuss the matter further during the MLA convention. He agreed to do so.

Soon after Ed called, our faculty secretary gave me a message from Tom Taylor, who said he was an associate of Del Knowler at Corporation S. They told her that they would type and scan our data for around $25,000, about 10% less than Dissly's bid for taking it right off the printed page. A letter from Compuscan also arrived, quoting a price of $38,000, but it wasn't clear to me whether they assumed direct scanning or typing first and then scanning. I wrote for clarification.

As Christmas 1970 drew near, I began drawing together the facts for a progress report to the Advisory Board, which was now scheduled for the 30th of December at Dean Stone's house in Washington Square. In order to show what Will had accomplished I thought I would try my hand at a flowchart. In my investigations I had seen many and deciphered a few; they were computer men's own form

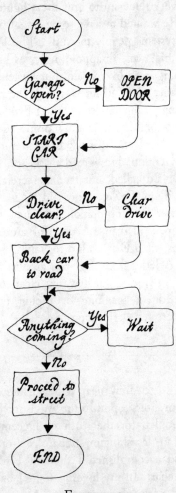

FIGURE 3

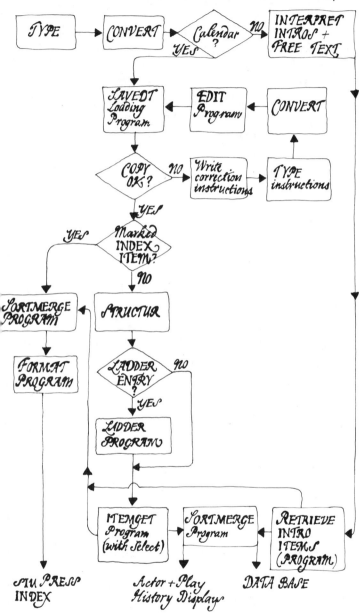

FIGURE 4

of expression. I thought them a succinct and lucid way of explaining a process, but I confess that they also held a certain glamorous attraction for me.

Any process at all can be presented in a flowchart. Figure 3 is a flowchart for backing a car out of a garage and parking it in front of a house. In this flowchart diamonds denote decision boxes, allowing for yes and no only, and squares denote action boxes. The operation of the system Will was building is shown in Figure 4. In this flowchart each action box is a job performed by a program. Data and a program are loaded into the computer at the beginning of each step and a transformation of the data according to the program is produced. The chart assumes that a given item of a *London Stage* performance entry is being processed. Of the programs shown in Figure 4, Will had already completed viable but unpolished versions of SAVEDT, STRUCTUR, ITEMGET, and FORMAT; SORTMERGE is a standard piece of IBM 360 software; LADDER, the most formidable of all, was not even started.

I had thought that computer men are overly cute in naming programs, but seeing the problems of naming from Will's point of view convinces me that computing circumstances dictate most of the cuteness. Computer systems of force decree that not only programs but many parts of a program and every file of data in each of its several forms must have a name and that this name must be repeatedly typed or keypunched whenever a program or a job calls for it. Having so many names to write and remember causes programmers to abbreviate and to invent abbreviations that are easy to remember. A little joke in a name helps jog the memory. Will's names, however, in spite of temptations, were good examples, I thought, of that admirable mnemonic device of calling a spade a spade.

He was occasionally vulnerable to an impulse of fancy. One day, when he was showing me how to put our system on the computer, I noticed that the name he had given to the disk that contained all our programs was GWSJR1, standing for no less than George Winchester Stone, Jr., the chairman of the Advisory Board. "Shame on you, Will," I said. "It's the Boss Disk, isn't it?" he answered wryly. There was more true wit in this unforgettable name than in the pretentious cleverness of some well-known systems that come to mind, like SMART, LUCID, and LACONIQ, which really cannot be excused as acronyms of such patently improbable descriptors as "Salton's Magical Automatic Retrieval Technique," "Language for Utility Checkout and Instrumentation Development," and "LAboratory Computer ONline In Quiry". The last name lacks entirely that most important ingredient of true wit, a sense of difficulty overcome.

I have said something about SAVEDT already. STRUCTUR interprets structured (i.e., not extraneous) text and labels every item in it as a date, theatre, title, actor, role, song, singer, dancer, or whatever. ITEMGET uses tags attached by STRUCTUR to arrange items in their proper fields ready for sorting by SORTMERGE. SORTMERGE sorts items in any field alphabetically or numerically, depending on whether it's sorting a date or name field; it can sort items in all fields at once in a hierarchical order. FORMAT prints the resulting display. LADDER replaces ladder references with actual casts, updating to allow for exceptions to the casts carried forward.

One interesting feature of flowcharts is that they can be continually atomized, somewhat like an outline. Each action box in a flowchart can itself be broken up into a flowchart. The flowchart for STRUCTUR might look

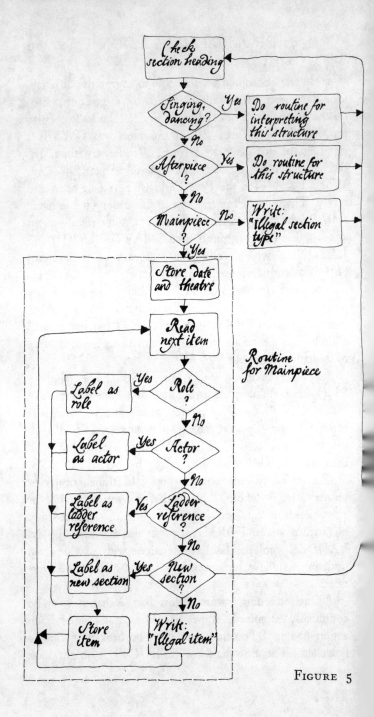

FIGURE 5

something like Figure 5. By "item" I mean a unit of a cast list like an actor, role, or title. Looking at my flowchart you can see why "getting into a loop" that it can't get out of is the bane of a computer's existence: because of a programming error it is unable to reach a condition that allows it to go on to the next step, and gets stuck. Each box of my chart is divisible into further steps, up to the point where each step is a line in Will's program, and beyond that to the point where each step is a machine operation. One word in a program may command a machine "subroutine" as complex and extensive as "build the house" in the everyday world. Will's STRUCTUR program in its final form was 600 lines long, almost as long as a book of *Paradise Lost*.

When the MLA convenes in New York its participants occupy seven hotels and its meetings last for three days. In the mad scramble that ensued in 1970, I was able to attend only one session of the several hundred scheduled. It was a symposium in honor of the playwright Congreve's 300th anniversary at which two of my favorite critics of Restoration comedy spoke, a quite remarkable coincidence considering that there are only four that I can really agree with. David Mann of Miami University in Ohio, who had just finished doing a concordance of Congreve's dramatic works, had gotten the program together. Afterwards he expressed great interest in LSIB and wondered if it would like to be the final repository of his computer tapes. I thought it a splendid idea. Adding the actual lines that actors spoke to our collection of facts about performances would be like adding flesh to a skeleton.

One reason I had difficulty getting to meetings was that I continued my shopping for the *London Stage* project. One day I went to the factory of the Hazeltine Company in New Jersey to see their new CRT text-processing terminal. The bait was that it cost less than $3000. The catch was that lower case would be implemented as soon as there was a large order for it, but they didn't know when that would be. I also had a good visit with my college roommate, now a member of a New York law firm, an important competitor in veterans' ski races and a better raconteur than ever. I conferred with a man who was going to put Alexander Pope into a computer. Ed Botsko of Dissly arrived from Easton in due course. He would not reduce his price or have a drink, but emphasized the near perfect accuracy that Dissly Systems could achieve. It seemed to me that we would eventually get our text converted for less than the $30,000 they would charge.

Our second Advisory Board meeting was squeezed into the last day; several members were on their way to planes. As we gathered, Emmett Avery's absence, alluded to formally in our chairman's preliminaries, weighed heavily. He had died three weeks before, only a few years after having retired: a few years earlier *Publications of the Modern Language Association,* our leading journal, had printed a vignette of him, a form of recognition reserved to the most distinguished scholars. "Emmett Avery," it said, "is a modest and unassuming scholar whose capacity for work and detailed fact-finding to provide basic materials for the use of his fellow scholars is nothing short of prodigious. . . . He is one of the drollest story tellers in the profession. Reserved and quiet, his sense of humor and of irony seems to come straight from the 18th century. . . . At one time he could give the arriving and departing times of all main trains at Chicago and New York for the whole country. . . . The British are beginning to learn how clear a picture of their theatre they are getting . . . as its records pass through Avery's mind and emerge from the wheatfields of Pullman [Washington] into the well bound volumes currently being produced by the Southern Illinois University Press." Of the five editors three now survived.

In the brief hour available to us we could not accomplish a great deal, but a few working points were established. Richard Golden, the ACLS consultant who had introduced syntactical analysis to me in September, had come along to consult with us. He was still in the midst of developing his generalized index formatting program to make indexes to anything by computer. The first advantage of making an index from a computerized text is that the machine compiles and sorts the entries. Second, with the aid of such programs as Richard Golden's, it composes the pages and sets the type by an electronic-optical-photographic process. The labor of human compositors is thus avoided, as well as the proofreading that their work inevitably entails. Richard was now offering his aid in producing our index to *The London Stage*. Needless to say, Vernon Sternberg, who had been looking forward to a photo-offset printing of a crude computer printout from us, was delighted with the chance to have a printing job nearly equal in quality to that obtained from Brüder Rosenbaum, but with a computer taking their place. The Advisory Board moved that Will and Richard put their heads together to insure compatibility between our two systems.

But we had miles to go before we indexed. Dean Stone reported his fund-raising activities. I quote from the minutes:

Mr. Stone noted the grief he had fallen heir to in his further solicitation for funds. To date, 21 foundations and individuals have turned us down. The Billy Rose Foundation representative is getting hard-pressed to come through with the promised funds. Mr. Stone noted that he had strings out to

Nelson Rockefeller, Albert Boni, and Mrs. Becky Logan. Allardyce Nicoll suggested an approach to the Gulbenkien Foundation. Mr. Schneider noted the desirability for Lawrence to open up a campaign for contributions.

I note here the irony of the fact that it was earnest of a contribution from the Billy Rose Foundation that had encouraged me to take the plunge. It was now conceded that not even a tiny bit of the millions he hadn't taken with him would fall into our hands. Thanks to U.S. Steel and the American Council of Learned Societies, there was indeed enough money in the bank to pay Will for the academic year's work we had promised him, but I might have to fire myself in order to make ends meet if something did not turn up.

The good part of the December 30th minutes was a brief sentence tucked into a paragraph called "Format." "Mr. Daland spread 11 feet of computer copy showing the banks of information and the varying analysis of these that he had made in a trial run." Something, then, a little something, had been accomplished.

———————————

Back in Appleton, at the start of the New Year, Lawrence's second term was beginning. I had planned to devote full time to the project during this period. Since we still hoped to match our offer from the National Endowment for the Humanities, I decided to proceed as planned. During the Christmas break priorities had begun to clarify and assert themselves. I now began to feel that we absolutely had to settle the question of how to convert the text in order to settle everything else. Each system of conversion implied a different set of Specs. Until these were final, program-

scanning of the text in the Dissly fashion would not supply some of our delimiters. If we ever found a way of converting Monotype tape I had no idea what kind of text it would leave us with. Transcription on a cathode ray tube terminal or the typing and scanning might constitute the economic optimum. For all I knew the MT/ST as currently in use was the best. It was time to pin down the characteristics and cost of each method.

I knew that the Institute of Paper Chemistry would charge $5 per hour for an MT/ST and operator. But I didn't know how much of *The London Stage* an operator could convert in an hour. Before Christmas I'd asked Byron to start keeping close track of how much time the girls spent on our text, but not to tell them, so that we'd have a sample of their ordinary performance. He could now report that they'd done 18 pages in 11 hours. Including the extra cost of converting MT/ST cartridges on the Digidata, this rate extrapolated to $26,000 for the whole job. The Institute estimated that it would take one girl two and a half years to type it, or two and a half girls one year.

On my return from New York, I had a letter from Compuscan waiting for me. The price they had quoted of $38,000 did indeed include typing, as well as scanning. But unless it included proofreading and correction, which the MT/ST figure did not, this price was really sky high. Compuscan would also scan one's own typing if it were done on an IBM Selectric typewriter using the Prestige Elite typing head. Their pricing for scanning only was complicated by an extra charge for the number of pages and a $250 "set up" charge, but it looked as if we could get the scanning done at Compuscan for $5300. In sum, if we could find typing at less than $20,000, we could beat the MT/ST estimate. Typing alone at Compuscan would cost $32,000.

typing prices was the cost of typing doctoral dissertations. Wherever there is a university there is also an unorganized cottage-industry of faculty wives, typists in academic offices, and local housewives who type dissertations at home. The going rate in Appleton was 50 cents per page. Allowing for the fact that a dissertation page is considerably shorter than a *London Stage* page, typing *The London Stage* at dissertation prices would cost $5800. If Compuscan scanned and dissertation typists typed, the cost of conversion might be as low as $11,000. I determined to run a test of the type-scan method to see if it was as feasible and cheap as it seemed.

The letter from Compuscan included a print of the Prestige Elite character set. Unfortunately, there weren't any brackets or quotation marks on it and our present Specs decreed brackets for extraneous text and quotation marks for italics. Of course we could use other characters on the typing element: we could have our typists use a ¢ for a left bracket and a ± for a right bracket; they could use a ½ for an open quote and a ¼ for a close quote, but there wasn't anything very mnemonic about that.

I thought Compuscan had made a most unfortunate choice of a typing element. I telephoned my correspondent at Compuscan to ask if we could use some other element with a better character set. Actually, he maintained, they'd had very few problems with this typing head. In direct but unconscious contradiction of this statement, he went on to explain that they had chopped a piece off the one to distinguish it from a small letter *l* and cut a hole in the side of the zero to differentiate it from a capital *O*. Now their scanner was reading these characters perfectly. The modification was extremely difficult to perform, but Compuscan's engineers had triumphed. I thought I saw them in white coats clustered around a typing element like doctors in an operating theatre. My correspondent would send me a modified element in the next mail, with Compuscan's Typescan Typing Instructions. These would demonstrate the utter simplicity of the whole process.

Then, on the cold and dim afternoon of the 7th of January 1971, I had a telephone call from John Chan at Foto-Mem. John wondered whether I'd reached any decision on CRT terminals. I asked him whether they were getting around to adding lower case, and he said they weren't. Then I went into a long and labored explanation of why I wanted lower as well as upper case, and told him all about *The London Stage*. "Ben," he said, "you don't need my terminal. What you need is my keypunching service." "Keypunching," I said. "What do I want that for? Keypunching is for accounts and payrolls, not for text." "Why not?" he said. "I can give you a very competitive price." I doubted that it would save me from despair, having heard what Compuscan and the Institute had to offer. "How about $2.50 for 8000 characters? $5 verified." I calculate very slowly, especially under stress, but I soon realized that this was in truth a "ridiculously low price." I voiced disbelief. "We do it in Hong Kong," he said cheerfully. "A fellow that used to do it in one of our banks is in charge of the whole operation. He uses IBM training methods and tests. Only one girl in six qualifies for the job. We can guarantee 99.8% accuracy." I was drawn deeper and deeper into the Oriental data preparation whirlpool: if my ears misgave me not he was now telling me that they also did typing for optical scanning at the same rate. "Haven't you seen our ad in *Business Automation?*" John asked. China Data Systems was the firm's name.

After he hung up, I calculated madly for a few minutes. At $5 for 8000 characters John Chan had quoted a price of less than $15,000, and the price included verification. This process, he explained, meant punching the text a second time and comparing the cards automatically. Discrepancies would be checked against the printed book. "You have to verify when you use a keypunch," he had said. "With typing you can proofread." What if we had China Data type the text? The prospect was dizzying: was it possible that they could do it for only $7500? Did such a typing service really exist?

From an IBM representative who frequented our campus I got a copy of the November *Business Automation*. On page 32 I found a picture of a beautiful pair of Oriental eyes gazing over the top of an IBM card. "Meet the grand old man of off-shore keypunching," said the boldface caption underneath.

Cindy Luk [it continued] is one of our best keypunch operators. She was with us when we pioneered in off-shore keypunching, and she's still with us.

That was only a year or so ago. But so much has happened in the off-shore keypunching field since we began that Cindy is a real old-timer.

So are we.

And so are the rest of the highly educated, English-speaking operators in our Hong Kong keypunch center.

That's why we've been able to handle jobs for major U.S. clients of all sizes, from world-wide banks to retail chain stores, tire companies to international charities, both directly and through service bureaus.

Because our keypunch operators come from one of the most efficient and best-educated work forces in Asia. They average more than 12 years of education in English-speaking schools. . .

In the past year, our keystroke capacity has grown to the size of the largest American installations. . .

After all . . . when you're the grand old man in your field, you can't just stand still.

Right, Cindy?

In one year's time, it was clear, China Data had secured an expensive advertising agent. They also had a nifty logotype consisting of a perfectly round black sun with a small white D— in the center that succeeded in turning the sun into a thick C. I very much wanted this charming, clever, and cheap firm to be real, though I had seen enough already to know that a full-page ad in a magazine could well be 90% of a corporation's total substance. But if China Data did indeed exist, the cheapness of the keypunch might override its deficiencies as a transcribing instrument. The keypunch was still in the running, then, and optical scanning deserved serious consideration.

CRT terminals required looking into also. So many firms purporting to make these devices were listed in the copy of *Electronic Engineer* bequeathed to me by dying Viatron that it seemed impossible that they could all win a share of the market. My inquiries just to those firms whose product seemed good for text processing totalled 48. Reading the literature with which I became inundated, I began to see that the burgeoning of CRT terminals in the market came in answer to the tremendously fast computer's need for input and output devices that could keep up with it. Time-sharing was one answer, CRT's were another. The old mechanical printers, tape drives, card readers, and teletypes kept busy computers waiting.

Most of my 48 letters of inquiry received answers within a few weeks. It surprised me that not one of the computer giants who make CRT terminals answered my letter. Even by using CDC's free telephone number, I could get no results. A tape recording answered the telephone: it gave me 15 seconds to state my business, and promised to call back soon with information. I tried this three successive days without raising a human voice in return. Nor would RCA, Bunker-Ramo, Raytheon, Honeywell, Burroughs, NCR, or Xerox bother to reply.

Because RCA's terminal sounded especially interesting I wrote them three successive times at different addresses. I note without surprise that they have departed from the computer business. NCR replied that my letter was being referred to the proper department, and that was the last I ever heard from them. Some of the smaller companies were unresponsive, too. When I reached one of them on the telephone, it turned out that they were still designing the terminal. At Sugarman Laboratories, Mr. Sugarman answered the phone. The kind of terminal he supplied, I gathered, was determined more by what one wanted than what he had.

At the other extreme one vendor, most obligingly but perhaps prematurely, sent their man in Chicago to Lawrence—twice—to do a "demo." The terminal did lots of clever tricks by itself but refused both times to communicate as advertised with our computer. A middleman representing another firm made the trip to Appleton only to discover that he didn't exactly know what the terminal did. Another promising make unexplainably dropped from our regional supplier's line shortly after it had been enthusiastically marketed in my office.

Some terminals were called "intelligent" and some were called "unintelligent." One did not use the word "stupid." Intelligent terminals had little computers in them that could edit and do other routine chores, so as not to burden the main computer. When all the facts I could obtain were in, it was apparent that about half of the terminals on my list were intelligent enough to carry out an editor's normal wishes—to insert, delete, and write over pieces of text at will. But of these only six had full upper and lower case character sets. In their haste to save cost and exploit the keypunch market were they not copying the deficiencies of a medium which must soon perish from its crippling handicaps anyhow?

If the amount of text is small, the method of conversion makes little difference, but it would take 23,000,000
keystrokes (21,000,000 characters plus 2,000,000 shifts
for capitals) to convert *The London Stage*. A difference of
one cent per thousand keystrokes would be a difference of
$210; a saving of two cents per thousand would buy an
IBM Selectric typewriter. A saving of thirteen cents per
thousand would buy a CRT. We ought therefore at least to
test a CRT as a data entry device. Perhaps we could rent
one for several months. And since it was a text-editing device that communicated intimately with a computer it was
also a leading contender for the box marked "edit" in our
system's flow chart, for fixing text after it had been computerized. But we had no money in the present budget to
purchase such an item or to rent it on a long-term basis.

At this juncture, four thoughts sprang into my mind
and connected. The National Science Foundation was
wont to subsidize computer hardware at colleges and universities, if it could persuade itself that computing activity
in general would be served. Lawrence had more than
once benefitted in this way from their generosity. Secondly,
this coming June at Dartmouth would be held the second
conference on Computers in the Undergraduate Curricula,
sponsored by the NSF. Here, perhaps, I could see people
like me and learn things I needed to know. People who
gave papers would have expenses paid. Thirdly, the whole,
many-faceted question of the relative merits of converting
Monotype tape, scanning directly with Dissly, scanning
with Compuscan the typing of housewives or of China
Data, or keypunching, or typing on a CRT, or MT/ST
typing or several other methods known of but not yet in-
vestigated, kept my mind swimming with disassociated,
unexamined, and unweighted good and bad things about
each. Fourthly, a stated aim of the pilot project was "to
devise the most efficient system of taking data from the

page and outputting it in [computer] storage." Why not do a survey of input methods, write it up as a paper for the Dartmouth conference, and if the CRT terminal came out far ahead of all the rest as I was almost sure it would, use that for the basis of a request to the National Science Foundation for money to buy a CRT terminal? I could at least set my house in order.

The first step seemed to be to define the criteria of a good system as well as I could. Because these criteria will help to explain much of my future behavior I shall quote them here in full as they took shape in "The Production of Machine-Readable Text: Some of the Variables":*

Since it is impossible to predict in advance the kinds of analysis to which a text may evenutally be subjected, machine-readable texts ought ideally to retain every bit of information that can be recorded on a magnetic tape. Not all information on a printed page is communicated by words. Type fonts, upper and lower case, punctuation, and page format communicate various kinds of information. Format usually differentiates prose from poetry, for example. Capitals are clues to proper names. Italics often signify titles. There is a qualitative difference between material in brackets and material in parentheses. In dictionaries, indexes, and lists, hierarchical relationships are shown by format and by type font. All typographical conventions exist because they convey information. Insofar as a system of data entry loses typographical data it loses information.

If the system involves key-stroking (typing, keypunching), it must foster maximum speed with minimum error. Achieving both goals is facilitated if instructions to the key-stroker are as simple as possible. It would be best if the operator were asked merely to follow copy. But typewriters and keypunches often

---

* Reprinted with permission from *Computer and the Humanities*, September 1971.

cannot follow the details of printed copy because their character sets are too limited. Some system of coding must be used to compensate for the deficiency. Furthermore, some tagging of categories of material at this stage can save weeks of programming later and sometimes capture information that no amount of programming ever could capture. The best system will enable a clear and simple common-sense coding and tagging method that is easy to remember. For instance, there is no easy way to remember that bracketed information begins with a plus sign and ends with an ampersand. In the absence of real brackets, "greater than" and "less than" symbols opening towards the bracketed material would make much better sense.

The keyboard ought to have a character set that comes as close as possible to matching the character set of the text being converted, thus obviating the use of codes for missing characters or symbols. The device also should facilitate the entering of whatever codes are considered useful or necessary. It follows that the best key-stroking device is the one that best expresses the text being converted.

A good input device enables the key-stroker easily to correct accidental misprints as they occur. Ideally, it should be possible to correct a mistake at once by striking over wrong letters, or inserting or deleting letters, words, or phrases without having to retype anything that is correct.

Any system needs a method for editing the machine-readable version after it has been made. Even the exact magnetic tape "facsimile" produced by direct scanning would probably need further editing. Texts which use format to indicate relationships of categories of information sometimes fail to follow their own rules. Deviations that bother human beings very little may have catastrophic effects on computer operation. Rewriting of variant material will be necessary before programs to parse rigidly structured data can be written. It is usually easier to change a few places in a text than to write elaborate programs to deal with rare exceptions. Irregularities will also arise during programming. Processing will suggest new possibilities requiring further rearrangement. And of course, if key-stroking plays a part in data entry, the key-stroker's own deviations will be added to those already in the text. Efficient text-processing requires a key-stroking device capable of revising the already converted version of the text without any restroking of the correct material. For error correcting after conversion the editor needs a textual medium in which erasing is effortless and complete, in which writing on top of text automatically erases what is underneath, and in which untouched text expands to allow for insertions and contracts to fill up deletions. If no rekeying of correct text is necessary, making changes does not create new errors, text always improves, and perfection is possible.

As for the actual conversion itself, the purely physical process by which optical data becomes electronic data, the desiderata are few and simple: the mechanism should be failsafe, fast, accurate, and cheap.

Teacher that I was, I graded each device on the basis of how well it measured up to each criterion and then averaged the grades. As I had expected, the keypunch failed miserably and the CRT got Phi Beta Kappa. I have already discussed the advantages of the MT/ST over the keypunch. Far ahead in my gradebook was the typewriter that feeds the scanner. It was about even with the MT/ST in all but one category. It was much superior in economy. The implications boggled my data-processing mind. Every secretary, every office or home typist, by virtue of optical scanning, could enter data into a computer better than a keypunch operator and as well as an MT/ST operator. An IBM Selectric cost one-tenth the price of a keypunch and one-twentieth the price of an MT/ST.

Of the two methods that avoided keying altogether, direct scanning was superior to conversion of Monotype tape because the tape retains all the errors of the galleys and because the scanning program can enter some delimiters and signposts as it adjusts to font and format features. Direct scanning was theoretically, at least, the most accurate of all methods, not being subject to human error. But it could not provide all signposts and delimiters, and, as offered by Dissly, it cost too much. Apparently platoons of human proofreaders had to help Dissly's error-prone machine.

The CRT easily beat every keying device in every category but cost, in which it bowed to the typewriter. The screen of a cathode ray tube, when used as a window to a file of text in a computer, truly changes the conditions of existence for a writer or editor. Mankind now possesses a surface to write on that receives no indelible marks, on which limitless strings of text open and close like long freight trains to receive his limitless insertions and deletions, and disappear without a trace wherever he writes on top of them. The MT/ST can achieve the same result, but not without transferring from one tape to another. Because it writes on paper, you can't see whether you have done what you meant to without playing the tape back to your keyboard. You work in the dark and wait for the dawn to see what you did. Thanks to the intelligent CRT, I who have never typed an errorless page in my life can do it easily (within my power to recognize an error).

This survey confirmed my belief that I should push on with Compuscan and try to raise money for a CRT terminal. With China Data such an unknown quantity and with my need to learn more about the type-scan process, I decided to try being my own typing entrepreneur. A first step was to revise (and type over again) our MT/ST Specs to fit the character set of Compuscan's Prestige Elite type head. Their system allowed the typist to backspace and overstrike to make extra codes. Thus we could duplicate our red codes quite easily. They also had a clever way of enabling the typist to correct mistakes as she went along. If she struck a bad letter, she followed it with @; if she wrote a bad word, she followed it with @@; and if she wished to reject a line, she put @@@ at the end of it and the computer cleaned out the debris.

The lack of double quotation marks and brackets on the Prestige Elite bouncing ball was unfortunate. When 100,000 brackets are at stake one thinks twice before using ϕ signs and $\pm$ signs for brackets. But Compuscan's Typescan manual, I noticed, declared that not just the Prestige Elite but "most other fonts" could be used, specifically mentioning two fonts especially designed for optical character recognition, the "European OCRB font" and the "Underwood Perry font," both obtainable on Olivetti Editor 2 and IBM Selectric typewriters. One of these fonts might serve our needs better than the Presitige Elite.

I called the local IBM typewriter headquarters to inquire about OCRB and Perry font. The people in typewriter supply had never heard of either font, could not find any record of them, and did not believe they existed. Meanwhile IBM's communication network got the message to their salesman that I was in a condition of want and he called me. He hadn't ever seen Perry or OCRB fonts, had never heard of them, could not find any record of them and doubted their existence. I called the local Olivetti dealer. He had never seen Perry or OCRB fonts, had never heard of them, could not find any record of them and doubted their existence, but the regional manager for Olivetti would be visiting that afternoon and I might discuss the matter with him. This gentleman had heard of both and was indeed able to produce the character set of Olivetti's OCRB keyboard. Moreover, he would send me a print of Olivetti's Perry font upon return to his base.

And so, on that afternoon on the premises of Appleton Business Machines was unfolded to my delighted view, in all its simple glory, an illustration of OCRB "that meets the specifications of the International Organization for Standardization." Brackets and quotation marks were all present and accounted for. There was even an English pound sign for *London Stage* box office receipts and accounts. But I noticed that the Olivetti keyboard had one key (two characters) more than an IBM keyboard. Did Compuscan read the extra two characters? If not, which ones didn't they read? If, as they claimed, IBM also retailed an OCRB typing head, which characters did IBM omit? In a rush to get the character set settled, I called Compuscan. The switchboard girl put me through to someone in engineering. "OCRB isn't a good font for optical character recognition," he said, not answering my question. "But your Typescan manual says you read it," I remonstrated. "We can," he said, putting all the tone of distant potentiality into the word that it would hold, "but we don't. It doesn't work as well." "And the Perry font?" "That's not a good one either."

I never found out whether that was Compuscan's final answer because, having been blocked at every turning for a few silly brackets, I was beginning to get pugnacious. Impulsively, therefore, I made that very long distance telephone call to Corporation S in Dallas that I had so long hesitated about. In December Tom Taylor had given me a bid on a complete type-scan service. Perhaps Corporation S provided a scan-only service too, with brackets.

When Tom picked up the phone, he said, "This is Tom Taylor . . .?" with that captivating Texas cowboy manner that delivers a certainty as if it were a doubt. Yes sir, Corporation S had a scanning service. Yes sir, they had brackets and quotation marks. They had other nice symbols like a delta, a paragraph sign, and a lozenge, too. "You see, what we read is the Perry font? This man named Perry of Perry Publishing Company in Florida designed it. It comes in a regular IBM type ball. You'll find it works real well for text conversion. We do all the input for Taylor Publishing here in Dallas. They do all the school yearbooks . . .? . . . No relation, I wish he was. You talk to Mac Milliorn over there and he'll tell you how we do." The cost? "Well, Professor Schneider, for you it would be about 1.1 cent a line." After hanging up I worked it out: $3500. This was four IBM typewriters less than Compuscan, or ten Olivettis.

Without even having seen the Perry font, I hardened my heart against Compuscan and turned my face towards Corporation S. I accepted Tom's offer to run a test batch free of charge and he sent me typing instructions and an IBM Perry font bouncing ball in the next mail. The degree to which the Perry font differed from the MT/ST as set up at The Institute of Paper Chemistry required our first major revision of the Specs. Asterisks, dollar signs, plus signs, and percent signs took the place of the various MT/ ST red shifts (see Figure 2), making the typist's life a bit harder. But the confusing red brackets at least were gone. Moreover, she no longer had to worry about forgetting to insert the page number every time it changed. For, entirely without prompting, Vernon and Dean Stone had just now come around to our way of thinking and had spontaneously written us to index by date instead of page. The grapevine had picked up the word that I was looking for a typist and now a message came back along it to the effect that Dotty Church, wife of John Church, now associate high priest to John Bachhuber in the Institute of Paper Chemistry's subterranean computer crypt, was interested in typing at home.

Just then the whole world changed utterly. On the 8th of February, 1972, word came that a friend of Lawrence had matched the National Endowment's offer. Not only that, but when I called Dean Stone with the good news, he announced that Mrs. Rebecca Logan, the widow of William van Lennep, editor of Part 1, had given us $5000, and that John Merril and Elizabeth Knapp had given us $100. Like Wordsworth and Jones at the Simplon Pass we'd been so intent on climbing up it that we'd climbed right on past it. Our sentiments on finding that we had "crossed the Alps" were, however, much less complex. Dean Stone thought there was a good chance that NEH might increase their matching money to include the surplus. Now, instead of being broke the project had more than half again what it had started out to get.

I forthwith took off a week to write up and process another full dress prospectus to NEH for spending our windfall, and to see whether my department and Lawrence could adjust and approve as the plan required. For what had happened, it sank in, was that the pilot project might now aspire to be the real thing, if China Data were not indeed another Viatron and if I could be excused from my promise to teach full time in the third term. Instead of finishing in June with a report on how to create the *London Stage* Information Bank, we might finish in September with something close to the thing itself. It seemed worth attempting. If we could not convert all of *The London Stage*, perhaps we could convert part, and with three months more, Will might be able to furnish us with almost as much programming as our concept of an information service implied.

As it happened, the Endowment did not choose to stand in the way of this vision and I discovered that my colleagues could get through a term without me more easily than it was comfortable to know. Under the new circumstances input via CRT became purely academic. We could not get a CRT system set up in time. I would proceed according to the cottage-industry plan. I would hold China Data in reserve in case local housewives proved difficult to organize.

Like Julius Caesar, Dotty Church probably could write one letter with each hand while dictating a third. Besides leading a very active civic life she had a house full of children. When we conferred on typing jobs she paid such perfect attention to both the children and me at once, that neither had cause to feel deprived by her ministrations to the other. Another characteristic of Dotty was that she kept running out of stuff to type. About 10 a.m. on the morning after Will and I left her with the first ten pages of edited text and eight pages of typing Specs she called me up. "Anything the matter?" I asked. "Oh, no," she said brightly. "I just thought you might want to know that your typing is ready any time you want to pick it up." I could imagine her, sitting at the typewriter, settling quarrels, giving orders, comforting the wounded, helping with homework, while her fingers flew over the keys.

Dotty was using a special scanning paper supplied by Corporation S, with orange lines, invisible to the scanner, to help the typist avoid spacing errors and orange top, bottom, and side margins to help her keep the text within the scanner's view. This paper, however, cost more than twice as much as a good grade of ordinary typing paper. I complained of this to Tom Taylor, and he said I could use a number of commercial papers without lines as long as they were on a Corporation S list which he would forward. A few days later, armed with this list, I visited a paper wholesaler in hopes of buying 500 sheets or so of approved paper for our tests. The salesman who dealt with the inquiry immediately recognized what I wanted, but it took him nearly half an hour to retrieve the facts from his and other salesmen's manuals, product descriptions, catalogues, and price lists. Yes. I could have Nekoosa Edwards Ardor Bond OCR Grade 20 weight for $925 per ton.

"But I only wanted 500 sheets." "That's just the trouble. They don't do a run of this special stuff until they have an order for a ton." Later that week I bumped into Fred Leech, the President of that wholesale firm and a trustee of Lawrence who looks exactly like Rex Harrison and drives the only Bentley in Appleton. When I told him the trouble I was having, he roared with laughter. "Don't give it one more thought, Ben. Just say the word and I'll have them run a ton for you at Nekoosa. You take what you want and I'll throw the rest away if necessary. Not the tiniest little bit of a problem." I was extremely grateful and wished that the other firms I dealt with had a similar spirit.

Thanks to Dotty's despatch, we had the results of Corporation S's first test run before February was finished. Our Specs and Dotty's typing passed without a hitch. After Will had a chance to get a printout of the computer tape that Corporation S had sent, I asked him at our next random session how the tape was. "Pretty good, I guess. I haven't checked it much. Oh, there's just one thing. All spaces are one space. No two-spaces." Since our programs required two spaces to delimit the end of a play title this was serious. It meant for one thing that the typing crew would have to insert a hundred thousand special codes. I immediately called Tom Taylor, hoping it didn't have to be this way, but it did. Their scanner was aware of space but did not measure it. So all space had to be one space.

This machine's failure to register meaningful space probably resulted from the designer's overlooking one of our unconscious assumptions about writing—that space is a delimiting character. It was one of those cases in which computer logic forced into my consciousness an assumption about the nature of things that I wasn't aware of making. Will and I didn't know whether we could get around the space problem by programming. Since we were in the throes of thrashing out the ladder reference problem, we pushed the matter aside for the moment. The REI scanner's space-blindness was not enough reason to stop testing type-scan conversion or switching back to Compuscan at their prices.

I began looking for more typists. One turned up under my nose—Ruth Lesselyong, who had been the faculty secretary ever since I came to Lawrence in 1955, and who had worn out many typewriters in the service of academic communication, doctoral dissertations, and faculty books. Ruth could type your letters, handle your wife's phone calls, and direct a book salesman while she discussed last night's TV with her assistant. In honor of her joining the project, we revised the Specs for the third time.

The *London Stage* ladder system was proving to be the most difficult programming job of all. Ordinary ladder references like "*Hamlet*. As 25 Sept." or "*Hamlet*. As 25 Sept., but Ophelia – Miss Jones" were not so much trouble, although allowing for the possibility that the title, date, role, actor sought for in the previous entry might be absent or spelled differently and providing a constructive alternative action in such cases was no easy job. But complex updates like "Smith omitted from soldiers and Jones added" or "Jones in place of Smith as a soldier" and many other kinds of updates for which the editors used *ad hoc* syntax caused us a high degree of consternation. The more we studied ladder updates the more variations we found. Finally it was clear that we would simply have to select one standard way of expressing all these variant forms of updates and rewrite all irregular ones to fit the standard. We decided to convert all the omit/add kind to an abbreviated form using pluses and minuses. The two examples I have given above could thus be presented by one notation: "Soldiers − + Jones, __ Smith," using an underline for a minus because the hyphen was already employed.

One day, carrying out a promise to specify all the

Ladder change codes:

	UNATTACHED			ATTACHED		
	Replace	Add	Delete	Replace (exactly any actor and role)	Add	Delete
Role	—	$c-;$	$\_c;$	—	$+c_1-c_2;$	$-c_1-c_2;$
Actor	—	$c;$	$-c;$	$c_1-c_2;$ *	$c_1+c_2;$	$c_1-c_2;$
Group	—	—	$c-\_;$ or $c\_;$	—	—	—

c = character string

* In '$c_1-c_2;$' case if no matching role is found then the group is added.

FIGURE 6

forms the omit/add ladder updates could take, I offered Will three: a role plus or minus one of its actors, the deletion of a role, or the addition of a role and its actor. "That's all, is it," he stated. "All that I know of," I said. I felt confident from my knowledge of *The London Stage* that there weren't any more. The next day Will presented me with a chart (Figure 6), saying, "Here are the logical possibilities." By "attached" he meant those updates in which a complete cast group consisting of a role or roles was attached to an actor or actors. By "unattached" he meant those updates consisting of a role or an actor only, as in "2nd Gravedigger omitted." There were not three but eleven possibilities.

It was hard for my fact-oriented mind to convert these logical possibilities to casting alterations in the theatrical conditions of existence, but as the chart began to sink in I began to see its relationship to reality. I could see, for instance, that subtracting a cast group by specifying the removal of an unattached actor or role would normally occur. But adding a cast group by specifying a single actor or role hardly could. "As 24 Sept., but Nurse omitted," was theatrically true, but "As 24 Sept., but add Mrs. Jones," was impossible, as if an actor always carries a role around with him on his back. However, seven of Will's categories were probable in a world in which one actor could play several roles and several actors could be lumped under one role. This was four more than I'd been able to imagine by depending on experience. This episode is an example of how computer methods, by imposing logic, increase one's comprehension of one's subject. And that is why Will, who never studied it for an hour, could teach me something about theatre history.

———————————————

March, punctuated by a long-promised family excursion to Aspen, was devoted to such discoveries as these, while Will's programs probed deeper and deeper into the unmapped fringes of *The London Stage* territory, and I underwent the experience of being an office manager of an office with the area of Appleton and a population of two. Explaining Specs, delivering typewriters, providing a courier service for copy and supplies, scheduling, accounting, personnel, payroll, purchasing, shipping and receiving occupied me continually.

In the mountains of Colorado I saw ten thousand condominiums trying hard to look as if they weren't and I saw a score of scruffy teenagers of both sexes, stoned out of their minds, skiing straight down a face ugly and steep enough to turn Jean-Claude Killy's face white, often purposely on one foot or no feet, eerily screaming, without serious disaster or much success.

I could also see on the horizon before me, more clearly than hitherto, three giant landmarks: The meeting set for April 23rd and 24th at Lawrence University of the *London Stage* Advisory Board, my departure for England on the 18th of August, and the termination of Will's appointment on the 31st of August. On the 23rd of April we must present for approval our plan for converting *The London Stage* and demonstrate concrete programming progress, by the 18th of August the conversion process must be self-supervising, and by the 31st of August I hoped that the *London Stage* Information Bank would be launched, if not commissioned.

The last deadline, now only five months away, had the most menacing outlines, so menacing indeed that I despaired of setting up my own typing enterprise. Part-time typing would be slow. Only by increasing the number of typists could the process be speeded up, and that meant lots of typewriters and thoroughgoing organization. I now realized also that typing for the computer, however much one tried to simplify, was still much harder than typing dissertations, because it required the typist to perform so many operations that seemed arbitrary and meaningless. Without its own manager the typing operation could hardly be self-supervising. What person with the skill and experience to manage it could take a short-term job for what I might be able to pay? But I was now committed to converting the whole *London Stage*. China Data had to be looked into.

Most distressingly, after two and one-half months I still did not have the letter of quotation for typing *The London Stage* that John Chan had agreed on the phone to send me. Cindy Luk was beginning to seem more and more like an adman's dream. On the chance that there was a more hopeful explanation, I phoned John Chan at Foto-Mem. He wasn't there. Every day for about three days I repeated the call, and every day the telephonists who answered told me that he was not in but they would leave a message for him to call me. Finally one of them vouchsafed, "You know he's not with Foto-Mem now." So I tried the New York number in the China Data ad. On the other end of the wire a tired voice said that one of "them" would call back. When after a day I hadn't heard anything, I turned in desperation to my final resource. The IBM card that Cindy Luk held in front of her nose in the ad had a telephone number on it. By now I had only a Xerox copy of the ad, but I could decipher "CHINA D TA SY TEMS CORPORATION 47 MACA TH R ROAD, WELLESL Y, MASS. 617-23 -3 22. As luck would have it, though some of the numbers were illegible, the holes in the card were not. The number was 617-237-3422. When I dialled this one, a most pleasant young woman who was quite well acquainted with the plans and whereabouts of John Chan answered and said that she would gladly see that he called me as soon as he came in (or did she say home?), which he shortly did. Oh, no, he hadn't forgotten me. Oh yes, they could do it for the prices he'd quoted me before. With this confirmation, I decided to asume that China Data was substantial until proved otherwise, even though its corporation or body had ethereal elements. The initiative now shifted to China Data, but several days still brought no letter of quotation from John Chan.

At this point, without further prompting from the tired voice, I received a call from David Shiu, Vice-President Sales. Traces of David's Hong Kong origin, not discernible in John Chan, came over the phone, though even listening to him, I could not get rid of my image of the slangy, familiar Americanized Chinese that Milton Caniff used to create in Terry and the Pirates. I expressed to David my wish to proceed to some agreement with China Data and wondered whether I should continue to look to John Chan as my agent. David seemed to be fully aware of the position of affairs *vis à vis* John. "Well, Mr. Schneider, really it's better to deal with us. We're the same company and anyhow we arrange everything with Hong Kong here." I told him that if it was all right with him it was all right with me. I briefly described my concept of the *London Stage* job and expressed a preference for doing it by OCR instead of keypunch. How much would it cost? He rejoined "OCR is $2.50 for 7000 keystrokes, and we guarantee 98% accuracy, but I will have to study your typing rules before I can be sure. Is that the price John Chan quoted you?" I thought it might be a little higher but David rejected the thought: "That's our price for OCR. It has to be." As soon as he had our typing instructions, he would get a

letter in the mail confirming this quotation. Having duly
sent these, I received the following letter dated the 27th of
March:

In confirmation of your correspondence and telephone conversations with Mr. John Chan, we are happy to quote you a
price of $2.50/7000 key depressions for your job *The Lon-
don Stage*. This quote is exclusive of freight and we understand that you wish us to use your own OCR balls and special
paper to be sent along with the source material. Each key
depression represents 1 depression on the keyboard, hence,
spaces will be counted as 1 depression, upper case letters as 2
etc.

The turnaround time will be a maximum of 4 months although we do not anticipate the job taking longer than two
and a half.

As far as errors in typing is concerned, we can guarantee an
accuracy of 98% or more. However, the typing instructions
seem to be very confusing. We would appreciate knowing
whether these are the final instructions for typing or whether
there are changes. More examples showing the different types
of source material that can arise will also be very helpful.
As far as following the typing instructions is concerned, we are
slightly reluctant to quote the 98% accuracy rate unless the
instructions are made more explicit.

We are very anxious to be of service to you and the university
and we are looking forward to your reply to our quote and the
problem mentioned."

In the upper lefthand corner floated the big black
C-like sun with a small D— in it. And every quirk of syntax
was teleological proof of China Data's existence. True, the
price was a bit higher than unverified keypunching as
quoted by John Chan, but at $2.50 for 7000 keystrokes,
the price for the whole job would be only $8300, as
opposed to $15,000 for keypunch and verify. But we
would have proofreading instead of verifying. With scanning at Corporation S for $3500, we might convert the
text for $12,000, allowing $200 for shipping. And 98%

accuracy meant, I was relieved to discover from David, no more than two lines containing errors in each 100 lines, not, as I had at first feared, two characters wrong in each 100, which would allow as many as 20 errors per page. Even more authentication of China Data's solidity might be obtained. David told me that Gates Rubber Company in Denver, American Express in New York, Daylin Department Stores in California, and Scandata in New York had used their service, and he had urged me to write or call them for references.

I wrote, wanting the ocular proof for myself and written words to show the Advisory Board. Enthusiastic replies came back instantly, but there were two little warning flags among the bouquets. One response noted, "Very detailed instructions are necessary for them to do the work." Another said, "They were a little late in delivering." I had no doubt that our eight pages of Specs would be detailed enough, although they might well confuse because they still retained some traces of MT/ST perspective. And since China Data estimated two and one-half months and not longer than four, perhaps they were giving leeway for more than "a little" lateness.

I don't remember why, but I called China Data's Scandata client instead of writing him. Perhaps it was because, having an imperfect address, I availed myself of Bell Telephone's excellent information retrieval services. I was surprised, actually, to discover a Scandata office in New York, because my original inquiry to them in December had been referred to Dissly Systems, so that no inkling of other branches had come to me. Like the rest, Mr. Freund at Scandata in New York had an unshakable faith in China Data, and we drifted to the topic of scanning. His office was not, after all, a service bureau, for those who needed scanning done; it was a sales office for the Scandata scanner. Suddenly, out of a clear blue sky, if ever that phrase was meaningful, Mr. Freund dropped this question: "Have you tried ICI in Kansas City?" "ICI," I replied, flatfootedly. "Information Control Incorporated. It's a Scandata Service Bureau. I think they're looking for business. In fact I know they are. You try ICI." Kansas City, Kansas, was nearer to Appleton than Dallas.

I was dialling them before I knew it and was soon talking to Gerry Dowdy. "Rhymes with apple pan," he chuckled. About business matters he did not joke but was circumspect, deliberate, and given to thoughtful silences. I began, "I am the director of a project with the job of putting 21,000,000 characters into a computer. Mr. Freund of the Scandata office in New York said that you might be interested in scanning typescript for me." "I think we might be," said Gerry. I ticked off my needs: upper and lower case, one and two spaces distinguished, brackets, quotation marks, Perry font, guaranteed error rate. "Hold on," he said, "We don't read Perry font." When I asked him what they did read there was a silence, and then he said, "OCRB." Having seen Olivetti's version of this font, I could tell him that this would do splendidly, provided that there were brackets and quotation marks. He assured me that there were. What about spacing? Could they read a double space? Silence. "I'll have to check on that and let you know. But I think we have a way of doing that." Did we have to use a special grade of OCR paper? "Oh no. Any decent grade of 20 weight paper will work on our machine." And the price? Another silence. "Somewhere between 15 and 21 cents per page." Further examination brought forth the fact that a line could have 75 characters in it and a page could have 30 lines. At this rate, Gerry's top figure produced a total cost of $2100 for scanning.

I was stupefied. In my whole life I had never known the same commodity to be sold for four perfectly unrelated prices. If I could buy four cans of Campbell's tomato soup at four stores in the same country for 80, 50, 30, and 20 cents, it would signify a state of economic breakdown. What a coincidence that the last bid was always the cheapest! It was apparently not a case of less service for less money, because all four services guaranteed an infinitesimal rate of error. I did not expect, however, that anyone would now beat ICI's rock bottom price. With some anticipatory quickening of the pulses I sensed that the time for shopping and testing was over and that the time for buying and using had begun. I would soon embark on irreversible courses of action. There would be no more Prufrockian "decisions and revisions which a moment would reverse"; I was about to experience "the awful daring of a moment's surrender which an age of prudence can never retract."

With China Data and ICI doing the job, the bill would come to about $10,400. If there really were three volumes on Monotype tape in Vienna, they would have to be converted for $3000 to equal this rate per page, and the product would integrate poorly with that of China Data and ICI. Had not these firms closed off the Monotype option? And Nekoosa Edwards would not have to run a ton of OCR grade paper for Fred Leech to throw most of away. Gerry was optimistic about the spacing. But most of all, the OCRB font far outshone the Perry for text transcribing. In the Perry font, the small *g, p, q, j,* and *y* stand on top of the line instead of descending below it as descending letters should, and the tail of the small *g* curls the wrong way, so that to the human eye it looks just like a small *e*. Dotty had found that copy typed in this font had a maddening way of looking wrong when it was right and right when it was wrong. This would not facilitate proofreading. OCRB, though plain, was handsome (Figure 7), and all the characters retained their familiar features.

```
+ * / @ £ $ & ! ( )  _ ?
1 2 3 4 5 6 7 8 9 0 = =

Q W E R T Y U I O P [
q w e r t y u i o p ]

A S D F G H J K L : "
a s d f g h j k l ;  '

Z X C V B N M , . %
z x c v b n m , . ½
```

FIGURE 7

I made up my mind to have *The London Stage* typed in Hong Kong by China Data Systems and scanned in Kansas City, Kansas, by Information Control Incorporated.

CHAPTER V
OF INPUT

ICIFIX. Another Board Meeting, at which Reinhold is discovered in a Dragon. How the Burden of Editing was lightened. The Author decides to treat The London Stage *as a single unbroken line. The Author gets an Editor with a* quid pro quo. *IBM finds out that it makes an OCRB Golf Ball. The Author surveys his growing Empire.*

———————

W hen April showers had pierced the droughts of March a little, I had the brilliant but tension-building idea that it would be great to have the Advisory Board travel to Lawrence for the spring meeting. The Board would be able to look over and (I hoped) approve Lawrence as the site of the Theatre Information Service, and Will and I could put on a demonstration of the *London Stage* Information Bank delivering some goods. This would be followed by a cocktail hour and dinner to acquaint the local and visiting dignitaries with each other. The Board members and the drama department could perform for each other the next morning, and we could end it all with a long business lunch. By the time of this visit, the China Data and ICI input system should be thoroughly checked out and ready to propose for their approval. The programming system also ought to be patched together and running well enough to produce something fairly important. In a rash moment I told the Advisory Board in my invitation that we would try to search for anything they might be interested in, relating to the season of 1738–1739 which comprised our MT/ST sample.

Having learned from our experience with Corporation S the truth of Will's favorite corollary of Murphy's Law, "You never know what's going to go wrong until you try it out," I knew that we urgently needed to put a test batch through the whole edit-type-scan-compute process. I had also learned the value, after going through four versions of the Specs, of his guiding principle, "Get it in writing." Working on premise number one, I told Dotty to remove the Perry font type head, put on the OCRB head obligingly forwarded by Gerry Dowdy, and get cracking on a 20-page sample, using a hastily altered Perry font Specs. I set the date for the commencement of operations with China Data at May first. Long before I had time to wonder if Dotty's 20-page sample was typed, she was on the phone wondering when I would come and get it, and on the 16th of April I sent the sample to ICI. Perhaps we really could get the bugs out of the system and start serious typing on the first of May.

By now Gerry Dowdy had provided concrete epistolary evidence that he was not an idle talker. Further, he had consulted with his engineers and could assure me that the Scandata scanner could differentiate two spaces. For further substantiation I canvassed some ICI customers whom Gerry gladly listed for me. They had done work for Ed Burnett, Incorporated (mailing lists), The Old American Insurance Company, Southwestern Bell Telephone, Missouri Blue Cross, *Look* Magazine (subscription department)—all people who, like me, required computer access to long lists having a reiterated structure. They gave ICI an unqualified recommendation. Our bank also found out from their bank that they had a solid credit rating. I noted that Dissly, Compuscan, and Corporation S all serviced the printing trade. ICI serviced list-handlers. Was it competition with the keypunch rather than the linotype that had brought their prices down? with women instead of men?

By now Will had most of the ladder program working on the season of 1738–1739. This data would supply a decent demonstration for our Advisory Board, but there was just one hitch. Almost imperceptible mistakes in the MT/ST text could cause devastating failures of the ladder program. In a typical year, a play first performed in the fall might be performed as many as 20 more times during the season. A reference to *Every Man in His Humor*, containing a cast carried through the season, gave "his" with a small "h" so that all subsequent references to it failed to produce a cast. To repair crucial errors like this, as April 23rd and the Advisory Board meeting approached, we used a makeshift arrangement that I learned to operate to save Will time. Will devised a program that enabled you stop the tape at the place where the error was by specifying the line number, as it copied the text onto a new tape. Then, by means of the console typewriter, the one that controlled the whole computer, we could write in the correct version. This version then replaced the incorrect version in the copy being made. Will called this program ICIFIX (pronounced "ickyfix") in honor of Information Control Incorporated of Kansas City.

The only thing wrong with this way of doing it was that you shouldn't keep a half-million dollar machine waiting while a fumbling human being makes up his mind and hunts and pecks an editing instruction. This was not the way to use a 360-44 with 128K bytes of core, three disk drives, three tape drives, eight terminals, a card reader, and a line printer. You should put all your instructions on IBM cards and give them to the machine to process as fast as it can all at once in a batch. To hide our activities from the Institute, we did our dirty ickyfixing in the dead of night. This way we could also have the consolation that if we hadn't been using the computer it would have been turned off. What user of computers, if called to account on judgment day, could truly claim that he had never wasted his computer's time?

———————————

On April 23rd, when the Advisory Board gathered, Dotty's sample had not come back from Kansas City, but I was confident that ICI could do the job. From Chicago to Appleton one tiny plane bore the four board members who could make the trip. Besides Vernon Sternberg and Dean Stone, that important plane contained two of the new members of the Advisory Board. John Robinson, a Londoner by birth and a Glaswegian by education, was now a professor of English and Associate Dean at the University of Nebraska, where Willa Cather, Fabulist of the Plains, had once gone for book learning. He had joined us by virtue of a special interest in theatre history, bred while compiling, with another Glaswegian, James Arnott, *English Theatrical Literature, 1559–1900: A Bibliography*. The Advisory Board believed that the incorporation into the *London Stage* Information Bank of another source pertaining to the same persons, places, things, and topics was plausible, and John approved of the idea. The other new member was Cecil Price, a Welshman, professor of English and Dean of the College of Arts at the University College of Swansea, Wales, birthplace and favorite subject of Dylan Thomas, poet. April, 1971, happened to find him in Chicago, gathering notes at the Newberry Library of rare books for his definitive editions of Richard Brinsley Sheridan's letters and plays. Very fortunately for us, Professor Price had accepted our invitation and now, most fortunately, he was in striking distance from Appleton and able to come.

The first item on the Advisory Board's program was a visit to the crypt at the Institute of Paper Chemistry, where LSIB was to do its turn. I was not as nervous as I had been before my Ph.D. oral, but although Will and I had worked far into the night before ickyfixing the MT/ST tape, I had never seen this version of the system work, and I had no idea what would happen when we tried it. To shorten the length of the demonstration, we began with the output of ITEMGET, simply showing printouts of the data in preceding states of transformation. After explaining the printouts, with my heart in my mouth, I asked if anyone present wished to have the computer answer a question pertaining to the season in storage. There was a silence which seemed to me embarrassed. Finally Cecil Price tendered a question: "Do you have anything about Reinhold? Interesting chap, Reinhold."

Will had not yet written the SELECT option of ITEMGET, which would enable us to retrieve performances of roles by Reinhold only. But we could find Reinhold simply by sorting all records of a performance of a role by an actor at a theatre on a date. By sorting these records on the actor field and then, just for neatness, on the date field, we would cause all of Reinhold's performances to fall together in the "R" part of the alphabet, in chronological order—provided that this Reinhold had acted during the season of 1738–1739 and that mistakes in our data did not cause our retrieving rake to miss him.

I was relieved that the question came within the scope of our presumed accomplishment at this time, but Will, in order perhaps to show his software to better advantage, threw me back into trepidation by suggesting that I punch the "parameter" card which gives the computer its sorting orders. I had done this before, but not with an Advisory Board of eminent deans and directors looking over my shoulder. Will thoughtfully supplied me with the IBM SORTMERGE manual and found me the right page. There my eye fell upon

SORT FIELDS = (p1,m1,f1,s1,p2,m2,f2,s2, . . . ,p64, m64,f64,s64).

This I recognized after a short swoon to be a formula for making out the card. "p," for "control field position within the record," was the number of the character position where I wanted to start sorting my imaginary long IBM card that contained the performance of one role by one actor on one date at one theatre. If I wanted to start sorting with the actors, I substituted the number of the character on the "card" where the actors' names began for "p1." "p2" was the first position of the next kind of item I wanted to sort, in this case the date. "m" for some reason was the length of each field. "f," "control field data format," must stand for the kind of code that would be found in the field. I remembered that we used "CH" in this position, meaning "character (EBCDIC)." "s" was "sequencing desired," in this case "A" for "ascending," as if anyone would like to start the alphabetizing at *z!* Will also provided me with his own statement of the position of our sort fields. In a cold sweat I somehow punched:

SORT FIELDS = (141,40,CH,A,2,8,CH,A,)

Will put my card with some others telling it where to get the data, where to do the work, where to put the results, and banged out some commands on the controlling typewriter. The card reader swallowed the cards, the pickup arms on the disk drives thunked wildly for a few seconds, and (much too soon) the printer, with a series of short, tearing sounds, ripped out a sheet of writing, and the typewriter wrote a few words: "LNDNSTG JOB NOT RUN—JCL ERROR," meaning that Will or I had made an error in Job Control Language on those job control cards. The program had "bombed," as they say in our local vernacular.

Taking a brief look at the printer's diagnosis of the trouble, Will dived for the cards in the card reader and pulled out mine. "No comma after the last thing," he said, handing it back. Calling together every ounce of concentration I could command, I performed the Herculean task of duplicating and correcting a bad spot on a card. I was in a desperate hurry because I knew what could go on in people's minds when they have to stand on one leg and then the other waiting for computers to do their instant miracles.

I gave Will the new card. He again typed, the reader gulped, and this time the pickups of the disk drives thunked and thunked and thunked, perhaps for ten minutes. The thunking stopped. Then came a most beautifully rhythmic series of tearing sounds as the printer ripped out 56 pages of sort records, one line for each. Will and I went over to look. It was indeed 1738–1739 sorted by actor and by date, as illustrated by Figure 8. Then we all clustered around the printer and watched the alphabet go by in the actor column: "Beard . . . Griffin . . . Macklin . . . Raftor . . . Ray . . . Read . . . Rector . . . REIN-HOLD!"

He had played only two roles in that season, the Dragon in *The Dragon of Wantley* 13 times and the Herald in *Margery* 18 times. Not very much. I looked at Cecil. "Oh, he was very young then. Curious he should be doing a dragon. He became a great singer, you know." (Truly he wasn't very important in '38–39; I looked into a copy

a	1738	11	10	dl	Harlequin Grand Volgi
a	1738	11	10	dl	Harlequin Grand Volgi
a	1738	12	15	dl	The Harlot's Progress
a	1739	2	5	dl	The Harlot's Progress
a	1739	2	6	dl	The Harlot's Progress
a	1739	2	26	dl	The Harlot's Progress
a	1739	3	10	dl	Harlequin Shpwreck'd
a	1739	3	10	dl	Harlequin Shpwreck'd
a	1738	9	15	cg	The Dragon of Wantley
a	1738	9	18	cg	The Dragon of Wantley
a	1738	9	20	cg	The Dragon of Wantley
a	1738	9	22	cg	The Dragon of Wantley
a	1738	9	27	cg	The Dragon of Wantley
a	1738	9	29	cg	The Dragon of Wantley
a	1738	10	6	cg	The Dragon of Wantley
a	1738	10	13	cg	The Dragon of Wantley
a	1738	10	20	cg	The Dragon of Wantley
a	1738	11	2	cg	The Dragon of Wantley
a	1738	11	11	cg	The Dragon of Wantley
a	1738	11	16	cg	The Dragon of Wantley
a	1738	12	5	cg	The Dragon of Wantley
a	1738	12	9	cg	Margery
a	1738	12	12	cg	Margery
a	1738	12	13	cg	Margery
a	1738	12	14	cg	Margery
a	1738	12	15	cg	Margery
a	1738	12	16	cg	Margery
a	1738	12	18	cg	Margery
a	1738	12	19	cg	Margery
a	1738	12	20	cg	Margery
a	1738	12	21	cg	Margery
a	1738	12	22	cg	Margery
a	1739	1	5	cg	Margery
a	1739	1	9	cg	Margery
a	1739	1	10	cg	Margery
a	1739	2	10	cg	Margery
a	1739	2	15	cg	Margery
a	1739	3	5	cg	Margery
a	1739	3	8	cg	Margery

FIGURE 8

Gardeners and Wives	Rector
Mandarin Gormogons	Rector
'Masquerade Dance'	Rector
'Masquerade Dance'	Rector
'Masquerade Dance'	Rector
'Masquerade Dance'	Rector
Haymakers	Rector
Tritons	Rector
Dragon	Reinhold
Dragon	Reinhold
Dragon	Reinhold
Dragon	Reinhold
Dragon	Reinhold
Dragon	Reinhold
Dragon	Reinhold
Dragon	Reinhold
Dragon	Reinhold
Dragon	Reinhold
Dragon	Reinhold
Dragon	Reinhold
Dragon	Reinhold
Herald	Reinhold
Herald	Reinhold
Herald	Reinhold
Herald	Reinhold
Herald	Reinhold
Herald	Reinhold
Herald	Reinhold
Herald	Reinhold
Herald	Reinhold
Herald	Reinhold
Herald	Reinhold
Herald	Reinhold
Herald	Reinhold
Herald	Reinhold
Herald	Reinhold
Herald	Reinhold
Herald	Reinhold
Herald	Reinhold
Herald	Reinhold

of the *Dragon of Wantley* later on: the Dragon came out of a cave, roared, got beaned with the hero's sword, and fell over dead. It was all over in thirty seconds.) I tore Reinhold out of the printout and gave him to Cecil for a souvenir and I gave Dean Stone the vivacious Kitty Clive, and each Board member a chunk of printout containing the actor of his choice.

After this, the events following were for me more of a celebration than a series of meetings. I relished the pre-dinner martinis with the houseful of people associated with the project. John and John were there, and Dotty turned up in a smashing dress she'd made for the occasion that she really knew how to wear. Will wore his suit and tie. Dean Stone met everyone. My colleagues gave generously of social support. College officials graciously lent their presences. After dinner in the candle-lit banqueting room of Downer Food Center, Dean Stone stood up to say nice things about Lawrence and LSIB, and I, in a red-wine glow, expressed incoherent enthusiasm for *The London Stage*. Next morning the theatre department, with the Advisory Board as guest stars, performed well in discussion mode under the smooth direction of Professor Joe Hopfensperger, department chairman.

Our business meeting had two parts, one with and one without the participation of interested parties at Lawrence. The Advisory Board approved my proposal for the conversion of *The London Stage* by China Data and ICI. Lawrence agreed in principle to sponsoring an information service on a basis analogous to that of scholarly journals at other institutions, operating at cost or less, financed by fees from users. To increase British representation we decided to invite William Armstrong, a noted expert on the early part of our material, of Westfield College, University of London, to join our Board. In the minutes of our meetings,

Dean Stone emphasized results. I excerpt the relevant passage:

Professor Price requested the information available for the actor-singer Reinhold. Within ten minutes a printout was produced which gave date, play or afterpiece, role and actor, not only for Reinhold but for all actors at all theatres that season. One interested in Mrs. Clive, for example, could tell quickly from the evidence that she played 38 parts in 35 plays, and acted 126 nights. Since the parts were all spelled out, one could make a fine comparative study of her roles. The instrument seems fast and useful.

With April 24th behind me, August 18th, the day of my departure for England on sabbatical, now dominated the horizon. I had assured the Advisory Board that conversion would be complete by the 31st of August, when Will's tenure ended. If typing began on May 1st as David Shiu and I had agreed it would, four months would bring us to the 31st of August, and that was China Data's outside limit. But there was hardly any slack in the schedule for the operation of Murphy's Law, so Will and I labored to get the sixth, and we hoped final, edition of the Specs off as soon as we could. For we had to provide China Data with an unpuzzling set of input Specs in order to remove the if's from their proposition. I determined that these next ones would be definitive.

Working with Ruth, Dotty, and the MT/ST girls, I had reached several conclusions: 1) A typist could not be expected to transcribe from the book and bring all text into line with the ideal syntax required by our programs at the same time. 2) She could however follow standing orders to execute some of the most frequently required changes, as long as there weren't too many standing orders. 3) For more complicated changes she would have to follow an editor's instructions pencilled into the text.

Quite frequently, there simply wasn't enough white space on the page for writing in all the editorial instructions. In an attempt to get around this, I tried the traditional publishers' and printers' system, as presented in the appendix to my dog-eared *Webster's Collegiate Dictionary* and illustrated by that mistake-ridden version of Lincoln's *Gettysburg Address*. But despite considerable experience with dissertations, the girls found it very difficult and time-consuming to figure out the unusually large number of marks per line that *London Stage* editing seemed to require. The editor's job, too, was painful and slow. The bad parts of the text were so bad that the easiest way to deal with them was to cross out the whole passage and rewrite it, if you could find the space. Besides, if Ruth and Dorothy boggled at my multitudinous markings, what would Chinese typists do?

Cindy Luk of the enigmatic eyes now urged upon me a drastic solution. We would simply not do the hardest corrections (mostly ladder updates) in the typing process. Our flowchart contained and our system would eventually have to have a right and proper substitute for ICIFIX, using a CRT terminal if I could get one. This facility would enable us to rewrite non-standard syntax. We would thus evade the bother of explaining what was wanted, worrying about whether the message was clear, whether it had been clearly transmitted, whether it was received as sent and carried out as received.

As a result of settling for less, our sixth edition of the Specs came out in two installments: typing Specs for the grand old men in Hong Kong and input Specs for us. Likewise, typing Specs would have two parts: changes in the text which the typist is responsible for making by herself and changes for which she follows editorial instructions. She could be expected to present the date-theatre header in the correct format by herself, and she could also insert section codes and delimit italics. She could not be expected to locate index entries by herself, delimit extraneous text, or identify several frequent syntactical deviations. If we could find some way of marking these for her, it would cut our post-conversion editing task by 90%.

At our board meeting, after listening to my plans to convert *The London Stage*, Vernon Sternberg had frowned. "You know, don't you," he said, "It will take you several months just to turn the pages, let alone edit them." I thought that the publisher of *The London Stage* ought to know. He had edited it all once himself. Afterwards, on reflection, I began to see that editing might be a major obstacle on the road to the 31st of August. I couldn't seem to edit a page for Dotty in less than 15 minutes, and at that rate the process would stretch out to a year of 40-hour weeks. Oh, for an editing method that could mark a mistake and state the desired change at the same time. For example, to convey index entry delimiters with our new Specs using editing symbols from *Webster's Collegiate*, one had to put carets on each side of the entry, and in the margin put $/=/ for a name or +/=/ for a title. To change by these methods *The London Stage*'s recurrent syntax for listing singers or dancers to our standard syntax took too much work also. For "*Rule, Britannia,* by Jones and Mrs Smith" you must cross out the comma, the word "by," and the word "and," then put in the margin a delete sign, a 1/m dash sign, and a comma under a house so that it wouldn't be confused with an apostrophe.

Somehow, perhaps while I was wondering whether red pencil or ordinary lead was best for marking text, I hit upon the idea that the color of the marks in the text could indicate the change desired. Whether the difficulty of changing from one colored pencil to another outweighed the advantage remained to be seen. One could underline index entries in blue for a name or red for a title. For common syntactical changes one could cross out the offending language in yellow (so that it remained visible). The typist could have standing orders to put a $ before and an = after items underlined in blue, a + before and an = after items underlined in red, and to omit items crossed out in red. When she came upon words crossed out in yellow she could look at the word crossed out. If it was "by" she would change it to a dash. If it was "and," she would change it to a comma. I tried editing 20 pages of text by this method and it took me only 30 minutes. Changing pencils was easy if I held them close to the paper in my left hand, point up.

In order to achieve the guaranteed 98% accuracy, the typists in Hong Kong were going to carefully proofread all of their copy before sending it to us. Because the scanner, of course, couldn't read pencilled corrections, the girls would type instructions for our computer, telling where each error was and what change to make. When we ran a correction program, the result would have the guaranteed accuracy. This process also required a set of Specs, which Will and I must see to before typing started up in earnest.

Shortly after the Advisory Board meeting, I noted with some alarm that ten days had elapsed since Dotty's OCRB sample had gone to Kansas City. On the phone, Gerry explained that the reason for the delay was that there'd been more preliminary programming for this job than they'd expected. This was now taken care of and we'd soon have our tape of the sample. I wondered also if he had been able to obtain the seven OCRB type heads that

China Data would need. He said he was working on it. In New York, David Shiu thought he could get them too, if need be. After the baffled response of our local IBM people, I was suspicious of their optimism.

David also explained more of the mechanics of international data preparation. Pages of the text must be removed from their binding so that the typist could handle them easily on a rack at eye level. Destroying a set of *The London Stage* was an expense I hadn't calculated on, but we would have to mark all of the pages, at any rate, in the editing process. I was to send these unbound leafs by air mail or air freight to Hong Kong Data Processing Company, Limited, 21st Floor, Thai Kong Building, 482 Hennessy Road, Hong Kong, attention Mr. Harry Ho. Mr. Ho, I gathered, was the man from the bank that had originally set up the data processing service bureau. Air mail was cheaper, David explained, unless there were ten pounds or more, in which case air freight became economic. The reason was that if you sent less than ten pounds via air freight they charged you for ten pounds anyhow. Typed sheets would return the same way. Airport to airport by air freight, moreover, took only one day. Finally, the best way to handle payment was by an irrevocable letter of credit for about three-fourths of the total amount expected. I had never heard of such a thing, unless it was like putting money in escrow, as when I bid on my house. When the goods had been delivered, the money would be released to China Data. It was sort of like the bank was holding our bets. "Yes," David said, "it's sort of like that."

While going over the new Specs, my unbridled fancy, being so flushed with its victorious leap over the editing hurdle that it succeeded in shaking its reins loose from the hands of my judgment, conceived of a glorious way to reduce the price of scanning and at the same time lift another burden from the delicate shoulders of Hennessy Road.

Trying to establish an exact figure for the cost of scanning at ICI was difficult because it depended too much on how many characters one could crowd on a page. ICI allowed us no more than 75 characters per line and 30 lines per page. And they charged by the page. But it was proving difficult to put even 70 characters on a line, because we couldn't hyphenate without making the words unrecognizable for the computer. "Gar-rick" cannot be "Garrick," unless your computer stores the variation and checks every word against it. It was easier to tell typists simply not to break any words. But then, cast groups like "Romeo – Garrick" produced such very long "words" that typists would have great trouble predicting whether space remaining at ends of lines could contain them. And if they wouldn't, great gaps would of necessity occur at the ends of many lines, costing us money for space that could not be used. "Northumberland – Bridgewater" would cost us nearly half a line.

Pondering these things, my ungovernable fancy struck upon the expedient of requiring typists to fill every line to the brim, letting words break wherever the line ending fell. Instead of assuming a space at the ends of lines, the computer could simply assume no space at the ends of lines. If a space or spaces did happen to occur after the 75th character, one or two @ signs at the beginning of the next line could signify one or two spaces, since there would be no characters before them for the computer to delete. To make sure of the exact 75-character length we would set the typewriters so that the keyboards jammed on the 76th keystroke. Typists could forget altogether about the ends of lines and let the typewriter take full responsibility. With exactly 75 characters in every line, we'd save two hundred dollars, while absolutely eliminating end-of-line crises for Cindy Luk and her colleagues. Little did I dream what consequences this perfect solution would have.

At the end of April, being in Chicago with my wife on business and other matters unrelated to *The London Stage*, I called up my old friend Stanley Clayes, who dated back to our year at Oregon State University in 1954–1955 but was now doing the Shakespeare at Loyola of Chicago, and he came over for a drink. Among much talk, academic and non-academic, he wondered if a remarkable graduate student at Loyola, named Muriel Friedman, who was doing a doctoral dissertation on the prolific late 18th century dramatist John O'Keefe, might not benefit from talking to me about the prospects for using LSIB in her research. One thing remarkable about Muriel was that she was over forty. Since I thought she certainly might benefit, we arranged a meeting. She was a slender, efficient, and stable-looking person with neat grey hair and a very pleasant dry wit. She thought she would like to have a printout for all performances of O'Keefe's 60-odd plays from 1779–1800 sorted by play, then date, then role. How soon could I provide these? Thinking of all the work that stood between us and what she wanted and particularly of how long Vernon said it would take just to turn all those pages, I decided that now was the time to get me an editor. If she would help us edit *The London Stage* for the computer, we would convert the three volumes containing O'Keefe's work first, and we could probably give her printouts in August of this year. There would be mistakes caused by errors in the data and by ladder references too ungrammatical for the Hong Kong girls to correct, but the largest part of the material she wanted would be accurately compiled. "You have your editor," she said.

On the 6th of May Dotty's sample returned on tape from ICI. When our computer had printed the image of the tape, it was apparent that the miracle of mechanical reading had almost but not quite occurred. What we had received was not exactly what we had sent. @ signs sometimes read as ampersands, the double quote read as two single quotes, a line was skipped altogether, and worst of all, as at Corporation S, the double spaces were read as single spaces. On the phone, Gerry was, after silence, surprised at this, and upon investigation reported back that all these ills would be treated successfully by tuning the scanner a bit more. As for the double spaces, Charlie Yost, the engineer, had simply forgot to turn on the space integrity switch in the scanning program. "No problem."

There was nothing serious enough in this report, I decided, to require a change in Specs. I turned my attention further west. China Data made it a policy to begin every job with a 100-page test batch. If the results of this were all right, they went into full-scale production. The Specs were ready and I began to edit.

But we still had no OCRB type ball except the one from ICI that Dotty had used. A note from Gerry confessed that he had not, as he had expected he would, located any golf balls in Kansas City. "Ben, word just arrived from our IBM type, it will take 2–3 weeks to get the elements. Please accept my apologies, instead of helping you, I have only hindered your efforts to obtain OCRB elements. What should I do?"

Without much hope, I called the local IBM typewriter people, who I now believed were trying to humor me to avoid violence. My negotiations with the salesman went something like this: I asked him if he would be able to obtain seven OCRB typing elements for me. He said he would call back. He called back to report that he had never heard of OCRB, could not find any record of it, and did not believe that there was such a thing. I explained that it was a special OCR typing element, which might account for its being rather scarce. He replied that I would have to give him a number. He couldn't order it without a number. I told him that the number was 725. After a pause, he replied that as far as he knew there was no such number. I said there was. He asked me how I knew. I told him that I was holding one such typing element in my hand. Still suspicious, he said, "Where did you find that number?" "Under the lever you lift to put the type head on the typewriter." "You have a type element? Where did you get that type element?" Still disbelieving, he said he would investigate and call me back.

At this point I think I called Jon Hardt, IBM's ambassador to Lawrence's computer center. Noting from my tale of woe that OCRB was the European Standard font as opposed to OCRA, the American Standard, he suggested that I get in touch with IBM International in New York, the telephone number for which he gave me. After having been connected to a few more than the usual number of wrong people, I finally spoke to a young woman, sounding about 30—a bit plump, perhaps, but pretty—who agreed that it was her responsibility, if I really did have a number 725 OCRB element in my hand, which she obviously doubted, to find out how I might most easily obtain seven more. Only she did not at this time have that information but would call back the next day. I then called David Shiu to report my frustration on three fronts, but he was unperturbed. He thought his typewriter salesman could locate some OCRB elements in New York.

Now I was the doubtful one. In fact so doubtful that I called one Edmund Bowles, of whom I knew, in Bethesda, Maryland. He was the IBM consultant who had sole responsibility for the development of humanistic computer research, but he was, his secretary said, on his way to Lisbon, London, and Paris. I desperately cabled him at his London hotel, asking him, since it was a European element, to please try and get me seven and mail them to me, hoping that, remembering some previous correspondence about text conversion, he would find my request credible and creditable. The next day, too impatient to wait for the plump girl at IBM International to call back, I called her. She said that, Yes, there was an IBM 725 type element and it could be obtained from my local salesman. Soon afterwards Gerry Dowdy reported that his salesman had also found out that there was an IBM 725 type element, and that it could be obtained from the typewriter factory in Lexington, Kentucky. I thought a sufficient number of leads were developing by now, and told Gerry not to bother. Then David Shiu called to say that his salesman could get the golf balls from stock in New York in three days, that he had ordered them, and that they would be sent to Hong Kong as soon as he got them. Then our local salesman called and said that there was such a thing as an OCRB number 725 typing element, that it could be obtained from the factory in Lexington, Kentucky, and that he had ordered seven. I asked him to cancel the order. He said he couldn't. I said I hoped he didn't expect me to pay for them when they came. I cabled Edmund Bowles in London not to get me seven typing elements.

On the 7th of May, David Shiu signed a letter to me confirming his original quotation and accepting our sixth edition of the Specs as a basis for guaranteed accuracy of 98%. On the 13th of May the golf balls and the first 100 pages of text were sent to Harry Ho at the Thai Kong Building, from New York and Appleton, respectively, not quite two weeks behind schedule. I wrote Harry as follows: "I will send a batch of material every two weeks. If the first batch goes to you on June 1, and we supply 1400 pages in a batch, we should be able to send the complete calendar (7000 pages) at this rate in five batches, the last to be sent on July 27th. I hope that this schedule is satisfactory, and that we can keep to it." By now it seemed unlikely that we would transcribe the whole 8000 pages ahead of the deadline. By postponing the five introductions I reduced the task by 1000 pages and fixed our attention on the primary goal.

I now turned my full attention to editing. Fortunately, just now two more editors having Mrs. Friedman's excellent qualifications appeared magically on the scene just when I needed them most. During the preceding year several journals of literature and drama had printed announcements of our project which ended by calling upon any scholars "who are using, plan to use, or might use *The London Stage* in their research to please communicate the nature of this use as an aid in planning." Two of the several who had answered offered help. The first was Leonard Leff, completing a Ph.D. thesis on the late 18th century playwright and theatre manager Richard Brinsley Sheridan, while teaching at Northern Illinois University in DeKalb, and the second was Marcia Heinemann, living in London but doing a thesis for the University of Chicago on Eliza Haywood, a mid-century writer and actress. Both now answered my cry for editing assistance. In return, I agreed to provide them with printouts for their research at the end of the summer.

Having editors who were acquainted with the material was great good fortune, but they also had to know our Specs. Since I was a teacher and they were students and teachers, I acquainted them with the subject in the way we knew best. I assigned a lesson and gave them a test on it.

The assignment was to study the sixth edition of the Specs and a new document called "Some Instructions for Editing *The London Stage*," which explained how to handle the colored pencils. The test was about 20 pages xeroxed from the part of *The London Stage* that each had chosen to edit. After absorbing my comments on the test and after I had cleared up some ambiguities in the Specs, the editors maintained a very high standard of accuracy in marking and in the wisdom of their editorial decisions. I found that the neatest and fastest way to prepare a volume of *The London Stage* for editing and typing was to saw the back off with my woodworking radial arm saw. Treasuring books by instinct, I felt like an executioner when I took them to the cellar to perform this atrocity on them. [N.B. It ruins the saw blade.]

I put the matter of the letter of credit in the capable hands of Mar Wrolstad, Lawrence's Vice President for Business Affairs. The First National Bank of Appleton, who handled our finances, did not handle such things but arranged for our letter with the First Wisconsin of Milwaukee. David Shiu had asked for an arrangement whereby he drew partial payment for each shipment of typing from Hong Kong from the $7500 set aside at the bank, instead of waiting until we owed the full sum. This was apparently a normal procedure.

Now that production was under way, I turned to two other tasks that could wait no longer. The first was an application to the National Endowment for the Humanities for funds with which to finish up the *London Stage* Information Bank: proofreading the computer tape we were now making, programming for extraneous text and Vernon's index, adding the Arnott-Robinson bibliography of English theatrical literature. Part of the proposal, of course, was an account of what we had being doing up to now. Last month the Advisory Board had decreed the establishment of a newsletter, to keep the academic world apprised of our progress and plans. The second task, then, was to produce Newsletter No.1. After I had finished the Endowment proposal, I used the historical part of it for Newsletter No.1, typed, fittingly, with my OCRB 725 golf ball and printed by photo-offset. My 14-year-old son Nick key-punched the 150-odd addresses on my list, finding the key-punch, as I thought he might, one of the niftiest toys he'd played with for some time. From his cards the computer made the mailing labels, and my 12-year-old daughter Mackay and her friends set up a noisy assembly line on our pingpong table to affix these and to stamp and stuff the envelopes.

From the reflections induced by these retrospective activities, I began, with some misgivings, to realize that I was the ruler of a little empire, not indeed master of all I surveyed, not even really very much in control of the part of it that I directly supervised, but all the same having sole responsibility for coordinating the work of many people scattered across the broad expanse of the terraqueous globe. One sole purpose had called this empire into being: to accomplish automatic retrieval of information from *The London Stage*. Its main business was one editing-typing-scanning programming process, but this constituted only the visible part of the iceberg.

The process, to begin with, was embedded in what we may call the Universe of Research, because it is one, and it recognizes no geographical or national boundaries, not even the limits of knowledge. This Universe was represented in concrete form by our Advisory Board, who were ambassadors to and from the Universe and responsible to it. The project lived on the Foundations of this Universe, and could not exist without them. By announcements, newsletters, proposals, and reports the project made suit to this Universe for continual support until the day when it became an integral self-supporting part of the Universe, and able to live by compensation for its own contributions. In sum, the input process was sustained by the Universe of Research and had no other function but to serve it. The editors, Marcia, Muriel, and Leonard, who sustained it that it might sustain them, were microcosms of our relationship.

Each step of the process took place in a separate world, having laws and customs of its own: the academic editors, the data processors on the 21st floor of the Thai Kong Building, the computer center at the Institute of Paper Chemistry, the service bureau in Kansas City. And each of these worlds had bonds to other worlds that must be reckoned with. I pass over cities, states, nations, principalities, and realms, though customs and excise men must have their due. Editing, for example, involved the worlds of telecommunications, the mails, the airlines. Typing, besides these, involved not simply China Data in New York and Hong Kong Data Processing in Hong Kong, but national and international banks. Scanning involved not only Information Control Incorporated, but these same realms of transport and communication, Scandata Corporation in Pennsylvania, and the typewriter Division of IBM in Lexington, Kentucky. Computing tied in Will Daland, computer scientist, the Institute of Paper Chemistry, IBM, and other hardware manufacturers too numerous to mention.

When computermen connect two foreign systems together which operate according to different laws, but which if connected can serve more useful ends, like a telephone line and a computer, they first build what they call an "interface" which interprets the "incompatible" systems to each other. A computer-telephone interface converts the telephone line's tonal code to the computer's code of on-off pulses, and vice versa. I had not measured the incompatibilities of the several worlds in my little empire and knew not the amount of interfacing they would require.

CHAPTER VI
OF THROUGHPUT

The author sets deadlines. Disaster strikes when the Scanner cannot recognize Nothing, and the Author courageously modifies 8 OCRB Golf Balls. He commits Hubris toward the Mails, travels to a Computer Conference at Dartmouth, & hears John Kemeny. Nemesis in the form of the Mails again. The Author flies to Kansas City. He is introduced to the Mysteries of International Trade. The Crises of August the 1st & 9th. The Author & Family head for England via Lake Michigan and New York City. Further mysteries of International Trade.

At the end of May, Mrs. Friedman was deep into the second volume of Part 5, I had started Volume I of Part 5, and Marcia Heinemann's test had returned—a solid A. Leonard Leff was taking his test. My daughter Devon, just home from college and in want of a job, was taking her test. We expected any moment the return of the first 100 pages from China, and ICI's second rendering of Dotty's 20-page sample.

If these tests were successful, and the editing continued to cover the pages at its present rate, we should be able to deposit several volumes of copy in Hong Kong on or about the 15th of June. That left them almost three months

(11 weeks) to complete the job before the 31st of August —not much time, but a bit more than the lowest estimate they'd given us. I made out a schedule. Because the "Part 5, Volume I" style was cumbersome and confusing, I gave each volume a batch number and called it a batch. This also made it possible to keep the priorities straight, since we wanted to do the volumes in the order of editors' preferences for information, not in their actual order. According to the schedule I made up at the first of June, Mrs. Friedman and I were to send Batches 1 and 2 by the 13th of June; she and I between us must finish Batch 3 by the 29th of June, and Marcia Heinemann Batch 4 on the same day. My daughter and Leonard Leff owed Batches 5 and 6 on the 13th of July. Batches 7 and 8 were due before the 27th of July and 9, 10, and 11 before the 10th of August. Editors were unassigned for the last five batches but I knew I would have time for some of them and I trusted that candidates for the rest would turn up in time. We would send two or more batches at once in order at least to approximate the economic weight for air freight. On Memorial Day there was still a chance that we could finish by the 31st of August.

On the first day of June, ICI's second rendering of Dotty's sample arrived; Will printed the tape and brought the printout over for inspection. They had corrected the spacing and the erroneous character for @. But we noticed something we had missed earlier, that capital *O* and zero were both being scanned as zero.

This was unacceptable. Our programs were utterly dependent on dates; and capital *O* does not precede number one in any series of digits. Prices of things and box office receipts also contained figures that we would someday want to add; and computers can't add letters and numbers. Of course we could translate all the capital *O*'s to zeroes in our input program, but then Othello would be alphabetized under zero, which comes before *A* in our computer's notion of order. Human beings are never confused by zero and capital *O* because context subliminally conveys which is intended. However, nobody has ever written a program that recognizes context, and Will, however much he would like to try, already had more than enough to do.

I called Gerry immediately, hoping he would say it didn't have to be so. "Yes," he said, "they're so much alike in that font that the scanner can't discriminate between them." "What can we do about it?" I asked. He paused. "I'll see if Charlie's here." Charlie Yost suggested delimiting every set of numbers at input or programming on the basis of context. Remembering the chopped figure 1 and the chipped zero of Compuscan, I asked, "Can't we modify one of them?" "You mean chop a hole in the *O*?" asked Charlie. "That might work. We probably could read it with SWAMI."

I had read a Scandata release about SWAMI (Soft Ware Aided Multi-font Input) entitled "Unique Self-Teaching OCR Soft Ware." Whenever a Scandata machine fails to recognize a character as a result of some idiosyncrasy in its impression, a human operator, looking at an image of the unrecognized character in context on a small screen, can enter the character intended from a typewriter keyboard. SWAMI enables the scanner to learn a repeatedly unrecognizable character by storing some of its features each time it is repeated. After several repetitions it stores a sufficient number of features to recognize the new character immediately.

When Charlie gave the phone back to Gerry, I couldn't help asking a question that had suggested itself before now: "Gerry, has ICI ever done any OCRB before this?" Following a silent preface slightly longer than usual, Gerry said, "Ben, I will have to tell you the honest truth: we have processed very little OCRB. And when I say very little, I mean *very* little." I shall always treasure this reply.

By a strange coincidence, not two days earlier the seven OCRB typing elements that our local IBM salesman had been unable to cancel had arrived from Lexington, Kentucky, and were now sitting in my office, looking at me. If ICI's machine could really distinguish a modified zero or capital O with SWAMI, I thought I knew what I would try to do. But IBM golf balls cost $18 each. Charlie Yost thought SWAMI could read a modified O; if anyone in the world actually knew for sure, it would have to be the manufacturers of the machine. Fortunately they had put their telephone number on the SWAMI release that I was staring at shortly after Gerry's memorable remark, with the phone gently resting on its cradle. But not for long. "I am a customer of a Scandata service bureau," I said to the concerned young woman who answered my call in Norristown, Pennsylvania. "I have a technical problem that has to do with the machine's engineering. Do you think I may talk to the chief engineer?" She made no commitment but turned me off for a while. "I've found Mr. Jack McIntyre for you," she finally came back. "We think he can answer your question." The thing to do under these circumstances, according to Mr. McIntyre, was either to put your data in fixed fields or modify the O and read it with SWAMI. Did you chop a hole in it? He said, "Yes." I asked if I should take the hole out of the bottom, as Compuscan had done. "No-oh, I should think not." The side, then? Which side? "I should think the left, so as not to look like a C". Just a little nick or what? "I should think a bit more, so as not to get clogged up." The O or the zero? "Whichever you use the least. SWAMI slows down the

scanner." Mr. McIntyre had no idea how you nicked the
O. There were people in Hawaii who made special golf
balls and that sort of thing. If I did get the O modified,
would it work? "It ought to." I timidly wondered if there
were some special expert at Scandata who could reassure
me. "Well, I guess you would say I was the one. I worked
on the design of the machine."

I had heard of these people in Hawaii and of the three
or four figures they charged. Now every do-it-yourself vein
and artery of my body thrilled at the thought of the great
sum of money I had an opportunity to save and the great
glory it was possible for me to win, even greater than that
time I found the tiny loose wire on the motor winding of
the timer of the washing machine and saved $49.50 by
intrepidly soldering it to what I guessed was the right
terminal.

I had an idea for controlling the cutting tool. The risky
thing was what tool to use. The man at Compuscan had
given me the idea that the material was unbelievably hard
as indeed it would have to be, but that Compuscan's engineers had found a way to chip it like some Kohinoor
diamond. At the same time I had heard a rumor in some
office that if you dropped it it would fly into thousands of
pieces. At IBM Typewriter HQ Appleton, they thought it
was some kind of hard plastic and talked of Hawaii. What
could this precious charactered globe be made of, that
looked like lead but weighed less, when you hefted it, than
a ping pong ball? I have never found out. I decided to
grind, not chip, using one of those drills for making jewelry
that are about the size of a fountain pen. The drill might
jump and go wild like a buzz saw that hits the wood the
wrong way, causing havoc all around, or at the touch of
the adamant the grinding wheel might disintegrate, for all I
knew, or the O might melt away from the heat generated,

like plastics I have known, but $18 was a small price to pay for the chance to find out.

A colleague obligingly borrowed his son's pen-sized grinder for me. My idea was to clamp grinder and golf ball to parts of my radial arm saw and let it control the movement of the one toward the other, like a drill press, so that if the longed-for nick occurred, it would be where it should be. But first I cast about for a way to mount the typing head. On a typewriter it mounts on a post, and it seemed best to use what nature—IBM—afforded. After trying the ball on a lot of odd sticks and dowels that were lying around, I achieved the perfect fit (after just a tiny bit of sanding) on the pole of a flag of the size that little flag-wavers wave before they know it is wrong. We never throw away anything. So I cut off a bit of the flagpole and jammed it into the hole in the type ball. I fitted the other end to a slab of wood that looked about right for clamping to the sliding overhead saw mount to hold the type head firmly in front where the drill could get at it. The drill handle was oval in cross section and tapered besides, so I didn't know what to do to secure it. Finally it submitted to being fastened onto a piece of wood by a strap of tin can metal, punched in a hurry with a nail, that was just too short to meet the wood on both sides, so that I could belay it with four fastening screws.

I was now ready to mount the work and the tool. The type head clamped neatly enough to the saw mount, but because radial arm saws mount above the work table, the type head was pretty high in the air. These circumstances called for the shelf, six inches high, that I had availed myself of to convert the machine to a horizontal drill press. Now the type head was mounted on its flagpole which was sticking out sideways on the slab of wood clamped to the saw mount, as the reader may see by consulting Figure 9.

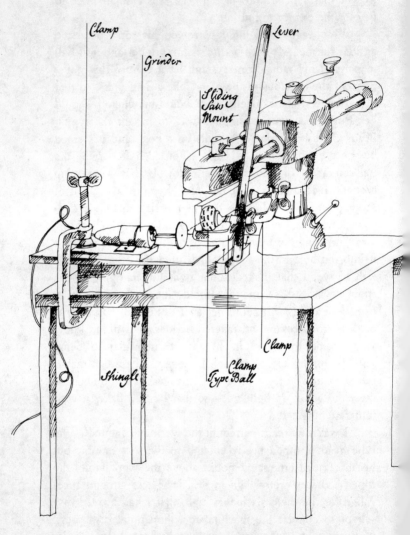

FIGURE 9

I was going to slide its fat belly, *O*-forward, gently toward the drill, which I had to mount so that its cutting edge would nick the left hand side of the *O*. Thank fortune that I realized in time that the left side of the *O* was the right side on the type head.

I picked a grinding wheel for the job that had a sharp rim about 3/8-inch in diameter. I thought this rim was thick enough to make a little bit more than a little nick and thin enough to make a hole so deep as not to clog. I clamped shelf to table and drill to shelf, with the sharp rim of the wheel facing the *O*. I now found I could make three adjustments. I could rotate the type ball to expose the right or left side of the *O* to the rim of the wheel; I could raise and lower the saw mount with its vertical adjust crank, so as to line up the axis of the wheel with the axis of the type ball; and I could adjust the grinding wheel's height by using a shingle as a wedge between the grinder mount and its shelf. The trick was to get the spoke of the grinding wheel in line with the radius of the type ball that intersected the *O* at the spot needing removal. If these radii were not aligned, there was danger of nicking both sides of the *O* or even the right side of the *A* next to it.

To prevent such eventualities, I also needed some way of controlling the depth of the cut. To gear down my arm as I pulled the slide forward I thought of trying a lever whose fulcrum was a block on the bench and whose load was the saw mount, attached via the slab. Four screws implemented this expedient. Tests showed that a fairly long pull at the end of the lever produced a tiny advance of the saw mount.

It was remarkable that you could tell whether the desired alignment of the right side of the *O* to the grinding wheel had been achieved. Sharp-eyed members of the family looked and agreed on which direction the type head had to turn. A magnifying glass provided a closer but not necessarily more accurate view. I didn't have the French disease and malaria and a high fever and I was not casting in bronze any snaky looks of a Medusa's head at the end of any Perseus' arm, but it was a dicey business, too, that Saturday afternoon as we fiddled and fiddled in the dank cellar, my finger bleeding from the tin can, children pressing too close, breathing too much or asking questions, in danger of open paint cans, broken glass, cobwebs, and falling skis. My goal was not as high as Benvenuto Cellini's, but perhaps the odds were as much against me. Certainly I felt so. It was not, can I make the bronze flow to the end of every snaky lock, but can I nick the type head in the right place?

Enough. I turned on the grinding wheel. It whirred. I pulled the lever forward, with contrary muscles tensed against the pull, slowly, ready to reverse motion at the slightest symptom of contact. The whirr suddenly became a very audible tone, in the neighborhood of high C, like a wet finger momentarily vibrating the bell of a glass. I threw back the lever, ripped off the type ball, ran upstairs, mounted it on the typewriter, and typed capital *O*. It was a nick to please the heart of Jack McIntyre. Except that there was a little nick in the other side of the *O* and another on the near side of the *A*. The position was perfect, but I'd gone too deep.

At a cost of $18 I had found out how to do it. However hard the type ball was, to the grinder's abrasive wheel it was no more substantial than whipped cream. For this reason, in fact, it was impossible to sense the commencement of grinding. A stop clamped on the saw mount slide might be the answer. It was, and abandoning ourselves to the machine's superior control, the children and I ran off the other seven type balls with lightning speed. In the end you could not see any difference between them on the typed page. That evening I showed Will how I'd done it

and showed him the identical backwards *C*'s. After squint-
ing at them a bit he said, "I could never do that." I felt as
if I had been decorated. I sent ICI sheets of paper covered
copiously with my handiwork so that SWAMI could train
their scanner to read them.

Meanwhile editing went on apace at our house. By the
middle of June we had enough text to warrant an air
freight shipment to Hong Kong. Batches 1, 2, 5, and 7
were unbacked, marked, and ready to go. At the Appleton
airport they said it was very simple. Send the package down
to Chicago via Air Wisconsin at the close of business any
day, they'd put it on Flying Tiger's Hong Kong freighter
at 4:30 that morning and it would be there the day after
next. (They reminded me that at the close of business in
Appleton it was already starting on the day after in Hong
Kong.) To avoid slip-ups, China Data's practice was to
send simultaneously a cable giving the actual flight number
and the airwaybill number. On June 15th all of these things
were accomplished and four batches, together with the
modified typing heads, were entrusted to the Flying Tiger.
This was enough to keep them busy in Hong Kong until
next month. Leonard Leff, Marcia Heinemann, and Muriel
Friedman, in DeKalb, London, and Chicago, were making
good progress too. A fourth scholar, Mark Auburn, doing
a degree on Richard Brinsley Sheridan at the University of
Chicago, had generously offered his assistance, and was in
the process of learning the Specs. We could breathe easily.

   Not so. On the 16th came a cable from Marcia in
London: "Still no sign of Batch 4 Always dangerous to
praise mail service Drastic action needed." It was as I had
feared, then. The nemesis of transoceanic communication,

accidental shipment by sea mail, had struck again. I had known parcels to take eight months! Marcia rightly reprimanded me for praising the mail service, for I had been unable to resist the temptation during the previous month and had indeed committed hubris. A better man might have done the same thing.

It had all started on May 24th, when I received Marcia's first letter, in which she, having read about the project in an announcement, expressed an interest and offered assistance. Only a week later, after I had invited her to edit and, in case she accepted, enclosed the Specs and a ten-page test, I received her willing reply, together with a nearly perfect test. On account of this remarkable speed I was tempted to forgive the English mails for having been on strike earlier in the year, and I began my enthusiastic reply, "When those English mails get going, they really work." I had set Marcia's deadline for June 21st. Naturally when she still had not received Batch 4 on Monday, June 7th, she wrote to warn me that the deadline would be hard to meet. I should have taken drastic action right away, but, not understanding the mails then as well as I do now, I just wrote her to cable me if she didn't have Batch 4 when she got my letter. Now she cabled me on the 16th, justly reprimanding me.

So I sent Marcia my own copy of Batch 4 to edit, by air freight instead of mail, on the assurance that it would get there the next day. This necessitated cabling her the flight number and time of arrival. But Western Union would only tell you when they answered that they were on strike. Fortunately, on a table in our faculty lounge an economics professor had dropped his *Wall Street Journal* in such a way that I could see an ad saying, "Call Western Union International to send cablegrams. Anywhere in the U.S. call (800) 221-7424 collect." So the message to Marcia was carried by scabs.

The affair was a bit sticky on the other end, too, as Marcia reported in her next:

I managed to pry Scouten [Batch 4] out of the hands of Sea-board—true to British standards of red tape they wanted a "waybill" number and for me to telephone you for it, but I managed to imply that a general communications strike was paralysing the U.S. and the book is now actually in my hands. I had to pay a £3 "customs clearance duty," which applies to duty-free objects.

Her bill to the *London Stage* Information Bank in-cluded bus fares, explained as follows:

Fares for my journey to the "cargo village," remotely* aligned to Heathrow Airport, of £2.25.
*Getting there involved crossing a roaring canal on a single log, without embellishment! (on it or by me).

Batch 4 had indeed been sent sea mail. It arrived three weeks after I sent it, at which time Marcia had already finished the batch sent air freight. I resolved never again to leave a post office parcel window without watching the clerk mark, stamp, and despatch my package.

On the 17th of June a half-inch thick package came from Hong Kong, containing the test batch and this letter typed in OCRB:

We thank you for giving us the opportunity to render our services to you. Indeed we are really very sorry for sending you the typed sheets so late, anyway, after this test run, we are sure that we are able to keep to your production schedule of 1400 pages every two weeks, and also, since our typists are now familiar with the typing formats, I am sure we will be able to produce much better work the next time. I hope the way I arranged this typed pages will be all right with you; and if this is all right, the next time we do the job, I can put more typists to do the work. I have also enclosed the copies which we have used for proofread, and I hope the copies will make it easier for you to straighten out any mis-understandings that may occur. We look very much forward to servicing you again.

Philip T. Y. Hui

This was the first I'd heard of Philip T. Y. Hui. Apparently he was boss of the *London Stage* job. The typing was good. Philip must have done a good job of explaining the Specs, but as might be expected, although there were eleven pages of them, they didn't cover everything. The girls did not realize that punctuation belonged outside of a name or title delimiter. Inaccurate placing of delimiters would produce some funny names. Also one of the girls consistently put quotation marks around box receipts in Comments, instead of using the perfectly plain parentheses in the text. Perhaps she was trying to obey the following instruction: "A long prose quotation should have a quotation mark at the beginning and at the end." Did someone decide that box receipts were long quotations by analogy to stock quotations or price quotations? We were dealing with a banking community. The next day these pages went off to Gerry Dowdy via First Class Mail, and I sent a cable to Philip, telling him that the sample was O.K. and to get going on the data I had sent, using the new type heads. At the same time I sent him a letter clarifying the Specs.

My paper on input devices, written during the winter, had been accepted for the Humanities panel of the conference on Computers and the Undergraduate Curricula at Dartmouth, and I went to Hanover to deliver it during the last days of June. Sally Sedelow, whose lecture long ago at the IBM-sponsored symposium on Computers in Humanistic Research at Indiana could now be seen as an essential link in the chain of events that brought me to Dartmouth, chaired the panel. She was still mistress of well-chosen words and few. By some accident, mine was the first paper on the first morning. I maintained that humanistic data processing was a special case needing special attention, basing my claim on the insufficiency of most input devices for handling text. Over a hundred, maybe two hundred people were listening, but they did not seem to be at all bothered by my great concern. At least I think that there was something stony about that silence, and as a teacher, I have faced a thousand audiences.

The composition of the conference affords circumstantial evidence for my sense that my audience was indeed not hearing me though my voice was raised. Only one hour in three solid days of talk had been set aside for humanistic affairs. The three humanistic papers had been chosen from a total of six authors. The other sessions I attended were totally incomprehensible, whether in physical, biological, or social sciences. The computer had drawn together a more heterogeneous horde than I have ever seen gathered for a single purpose. Raw mountaineers from Kentucky, Yale men, midwesterners with Harry Truman shirts, MIT professors with European beards, little men in carpet slippers, wide-eyed graduate students with briefcases, taking notes, anarchists of both sexes, and colorful Colorado families taking in the East Coast. It was science, not computers, that had brought them here, and numbers, not words, were their game.

Dartmouth's Kiewit Computer Center, which housed the brain of one of the first and foremost time-sharing networks in the country, serving via teletype schools and colleges all over New England as well as nearly every alcove at Dartmouth College, contained more computer hardware than I have ever seen in one place before, unless possibly at the Educational Testing Service at Princeton, N.J. But the system was not highly developed for text-handling by my standards. Editing of text was done not on the TV screen of a CRT but blindly, by giving instructions at a terminal to find a line hidden away somewhere in a file and do such and so to it. For their ground-breaking teaching network, Dartmouth had invented a new programming language, BASIC, which took full advantage of the fact that a time-sharing terminal can talk back to its user and interact with him. BASIC can even teach itself. When you request the lesson, the terminal explains a bit of the language at a time, gives little tests, and points out mistakes. At the conference, participants swarmed over the Dartmouth terminals doing things like attempting to land a rocket on the moon using a program that simulated lunar gravitational conditions, playing tic-tac-toe, or calculating the national debt five years from now. Dartmouth terminals were very jocular. When you made a mistake they called it a blooper or said you goofed. Wondering what they would say next made making a mistake fun. "YOU ARE HITTING THE MOON AT A SPEED OF EX-ACTLY 0276.20 MILES PER HOUR. BLOOD, GUTS, TWISTED METAL . . . YUCK," or, if the landing was a success, "LIKE A CLOUD KISSING THE CLOVERED HILL." But computers do not really have a sense of humor.

The most humanistic words I heard at Dartmouth were spoken by Dartmouth's leading scientist: John Kemeny, Hungarian refugee from Nazism, research assistant to Albert Einstein, veteran of Los Alamos, creator of BASIC (with Thomas Kurtz, director of Kiewit), promulgator of the Dartmouth network, and President of Dartmouth. To the conference banquet at the fieldhouse, he gave an address showing at once the atmosphere of number crunching I have spoken of and a true appreciation of the human factor in computing. He spoke (extemporaneously but without a wasted word) on three topics: The use, mis-use, and non-use of computers, in three areas—research, teaching, and administration. His examples had to do with numbers: "All the work that this team did in a year at Los Alamos can now be done [at Dartmouth] in one afternoon, and it can be done while a hundred other people use the same system." "You can't do a million multiplications in a second, but a computer can do it trivially." "There are 78,498 prime numbers up to a million. . . . It took me three and one-half minutes of computing time to find them." He told of how Christian Gauss's school teacher meted out punishment to him by demanding that he add together the numbers from 1 to 100. Almost instantly Gauss said, "5050," figuring out that in 100 there were exactly 50 pairs of numbers adding up to 101. By this example Kemeny was showing the value of the thoughtful over what computer men call the "brute force" approach to the same problem, that of adding 1 to 2 and 3 to the result and so on.

This was to me the main point of Kemeny's lecture. We are too often tempted, because it is so easy with computers, to use the brute force approach, to do more work to find out more than we want to know about the wrong thing. I quote from a transcription of a tape recording of the address: "But above all what I am talking about is the psychological attitude on the part of most researchers that it is either a problem for a human being or it is a problem for the machine. And I would like to argue that instead of a choice of human being vs. machine, the research problem should be solved by a human being working with a machine as a team. While a computer can provide incredible power to the human being, the combination of man and machine together is much more than either alone. I am afraid we are still very much in baby shoes. We must somehow learn to use the computer simply as an extension of our own brains."

After many years of looking in vain for my name on message boards at conventions I have given up expecting to see it, but I have not quenched my curiosity to see who the important people are with whom someone so desperately needs to get in touch that he resorts to this extremity. Otherwise I never would have gotten Gerry Dowdy's message to call him at 913-321-7902. I rushed to the nearest phone and soon got a line to him. "Ben," he said, "I've got bad news. You know these pages you sent us from China? They got wet in transit from Appleton. And besides, there's something wrong with the typing. The letters all have little tails. I don't think our machine can read these pages." I asked him please to try to read them just the same. They would, but he just wanted me to know that it was doubtful. So this was the kind of thing that got people's names on message boards.

That evening, I forgot about those ominous tails at the most humanistic occasion of the conference: a civilized dinner that Stephen Waite and his charming wife gave on a leafy green porch overlooking a Hanover glen for the dozen or so humanists at the conference. By a newsletter, appropriately named *Calculi*, by establishing an archive of computer tapes of classical texts, and by helping to organize a computer course for classical scholars, Stephen has directed the efforts of his computing colleagues in ancient languages all over the world along mutually assisting paths and prevented useless duplication of effort. One effect of this enterprise, besides easing the work of computing classicists, is that Stephen is no longer a member of the classics department, but a member of the computer center staff. On his front porch that June evening we were a band of brothers but, unhappily, few.

On my return I plunged into editing again, still harried by the vision of the grand old men of offshore keypunching running out of pages to type. It wasn't until a week later, when I received a note from Gerry Dowdy, containing a Xerox of one of the pages having little tails on the letters, that I began to think seriously that the quality of the typing could be a problem. Possibly bad typewriter adjustment was responsible. Scanning companies were most specific about this. "Multiple copy lever all the way forward, force lever on type ball mount set at three." I tried the OCRB element on the faculty office typewriter, and sure enough, if you pushed the multiple copy lever back, the typewriter put tails on some of the letters. You could tell why. When you strike a key, the typing element rotates so as to point the letter at the paper and instantly nods, hitting the paper with the letter. When you push the multiple copy lever back, the paper can lift away from the platen enough so that the letter is still rotating when it hits the paper. It therefore slides into the paper leaving little tails at its trailing edge. In their first 100 pages, Hong Kong Data Processing had used 16 weight paper instead of 20 and they were putting in one carbon to mark for error correction. Thin paper could bunch against the hold-down rollers when the platen turned in a new line. I cabled Harry Ho to pull the lever forward and I called David Shiu in New York about the paper. It was not the adjustment, he assured me, because they would never do that; it must be the paper. At any rate they would of course do the first 100 pages over again. He would ship air freight immediately 10,000 sheets of 20 weight paper. Meanwhile he was sure they had enough 20 weight to tide them over until that arrived.

It was now the end of June and nothing had been accomplished. Hong Kong's first 100 pages were apparently not scannable. In order to meet the August 31st deadline, they would now have to type at a rate of one volume per week.

I have never learned how to wait. When the wait is sure to be long, I can manage to forget, as when a publisher is considering whether to print my book. But when I have reason to expect that the one thing most desired could arrive in the next day's mail, weeks of waiting are unbearable. I do not lead a life of quiet desperation; I lead a life of loud desperation. Therefore, when on Monday, July 5th, I did not get a tape of the first 100 pages from ICI, after they had had them for two weeks, or any word that they had found them unreadable, and when I had no confirmation from them that the scanner would read my backward *C*'s, I knew that I would either explode or I would go to Kansas City and find out what was the matter. I set son Ben to work typing a 10-page test with the modified typing element and proper paper and told Gerry I was coming down with it Wednesday.

I walked from the cool plane that morning through the furnace of Kansas into the refrigerated airport to meet Gerry, who looked, as he said he would, a bit like a big Irish cop. We went back into the furnace, got into his red-hot almost new car, and began to drive around some cloverleafs while frigid streams flowed over our knees from the air conditioner under the dashboard, carefully talking about nothing in particular. At a Holiday Inn exit, we peeled off and dropped into a parking lot that could have served either of two buildings, one packaged as a motel, and one packaged as an office building. Into the ice cave of the office building we plunged through the volcano crater of the lot. ICI's premises were on the ground floor. One entered through glass doors to a neatly groomed reception room, thickly carpeted and presided over by a neatly groomed receptionist who greeted us with a cool warm smile. Gerry immediately took me to meet Charlie Yost and the Scandata 200. I now for the first time discovered that the machine's brain was one of those ubiquitous PDP/8's I had become acquainted with at DEC last fall.

Charlie stopped the scanner so that I could see how on a half-inch luminous strip above the console the character on which it stopped was black on a white field in a context of a dozen letters which were white on a black field. On the right was a two-foot-square panel pincushioned with little lights (1200) that were orange when turned on. This panel showed what photoelectric circuits had been turned on by the character being looked at. Characters could be slowed down as the scanner traveled across them, or stopped altogether. A space produced a perfectly black square. A period turned on a fairly shapeless blob consisting of several dozen lights. At this magnification characters that looked perfect to the human reader looked rough to the scanner. We were seeing what the machine's circuits saw when its electric retina received impulses reflected from its scanning beam, amplified and presented to its recognition circuits. A letter was recognized if a certain minimum set of lights in crucial locations were on. It was faster and more accurate to use only the most conclusive evidence so that extraneous flicks and flecks on the page had less chance of influencing the recognition unit's decision. Charlie fixed the computer so that he could go from one letter to the next by pushing a button, and we could see in slow motion what the scanner normally did at a rate of 800 characters per second. The scanner was busy with another job right now, but after lunch, Charlie said, they could run my sample.

Then we went to the opposite end of ICI's floor space to visit President Lynn Courtney, passing possibly a dozen office doors. My *Datamation* Industry Guide tells me that ICI has "1–25" employees. Nearer 25 than one, I should say. Lynn was a dark, handsome fellow, not much over 40, if that, and not tall and quite relaxed at his large desk in his fairly large office. He told of how ICI was scanning all the publicity releases involving U.S. Army personnel, and the Pittsburgh telephone book. He proposed that we all go to lunch together at the Golden Ox in the stockyards, to the bar of which he soon led us, after we had braved two bursts of Kansas heat with an efficient glide in his air-conditioned Cadillac in between. Once we were safely cooled off and settling into our second martini, with our feet firmly planted on the brass rail, Lynn said, "If lightning strikes once, you don't pay any attention to it, but if it strikes twice in the same place I figure that means something." We agreed. "First you come along, and you're a professor that wants to enter a whole lot of text. Then, the other day, a professor from Wisconsin University calls me about the same thing, and gives your name. Now you tell me. Does this mean something?" This call, I realized, had been a result of my newsletter. Gerry didn't know whether it meant something. I mumbled about the potential size of the academic market. Lynn never told us what he thought. If he thought that I might be getting ready to deliver all the English professors into his hands, it did not occur to me then. He said, "What I want to know is how do I reach this market." I suggested the scholarly journals, but he continued his quizzical look well into the steak and the third martini. Two dots of heat and a dash of refrigeration brought us back to ICI, watching Charlie scan *The London Stage*. I remember that I brought home a tape of Ben's 10-page sample and I think that Charlie also scanned a part of the unscannable 100 pages from China that had gotten wet and had tails, but this part of the day is mostly blank.

After that I insisted on a private talk with Lynn. I asked him if he would be willing to sign a contract in which ICI guaranteed an error rate of something like one mistake in 100,000 characters, which could include backward *C*'s.

Lynn put his hands behind his head and reared back in his chair. "I'm a lawyer, Ben, and I know all about contracts. You try to get it all down in black and white, but as soon as anything goes wrong you get into an endless argument about whether the error was caused by the typing, or the scanning, or the paper, and nobody profits. In the long run you just have to depend on the character of the company you're dealing with." I told him that these were exactly my sentiments, but I was leaving the country, and I hoped that I could have some guarantee that things like the backwards C would be taken care of. I had been told that the scanner would read OCRB and it turned out that it couldn't read OCRB.

I was dealing with one of the philosopher executives. He turned his chair and gazed out the window. "If there's anything I hate in busines worse than all, it's a misunderstanding. It happens mostly when you're dealing with people who don't have experience in the field. People who have experience know what to expect and these misunderstandings don't develop." I didn't know where to take it from there. I blurted out something like, "You have a big operation here and you're doing a lot of big jobs, but I don't think you're doing much for me." Now he reassured me. "Ben, you know we'll do a good job for you because we want your business. Of course we will. You can take that from me."

Now it was time for my plane back again. We swam the sea of heat to the car and from the car through the lava of the lot to the airport waiting room bar, where we had two Scotches apiece. One pulse of heat more and I had been properly poured onto the plane.

In the light of the morning when the haze had begun to clear, I tried to put it all together. Lynn was right about contracts. You couldn't expect to plug all the holes. Still it was curious that he wouldn't put a few things in writing.

What if China Data gave them flawed copy, with tails and so forth? How much would they put up with because they wanted my business? How much would I tolerate before I pulled out? Finally I saw the obvious part of it all that I had missed because of my academic preoccupation with principles: Equality, Agreement of Pronouns, Academic Freedom, Ohm's Law, The Search for Truth, and so on. Such guides to action did not apply. The main reason why ICI would consider my interest when it preferred to consider its own was that I was paying them. I didn't have to pay them if I didn't like their work. It was so obvious I never could have seen it without the help of the philosopher executive. Of course, my recommendation to others might be another incentive, but I hadn't looked like someone who was getting ready to deliver a whole lot of customers. What it boiled down to was that if they wanted my money, they would have to earn it.

But how much did they want my money? Did Lynn know that I knew that I could withhold payment until satisfied? If so, did he think the chances of satisfying me so poor that he was ready to forfeit the job to avoid the risk? Did he know I knew he knew he could forfeit the job? Now that I knew, at any rate, nothing short of alternative provisions for scanning would provide security, and the hope that he wouldn't guess I knew this, quit trying, and force me to switch scanning services at great cost. The conclusion I arrived at from my visit to Kansas City was that I was playing poker.

That afternoon Will brought in a printout of the tape I'd brought back from ICI. This time they had succeeded in reading our backward C as a capital O, but they were now reading the zero as a capital O also, and missing parts of pages. I resolved to investigate alternatives to ICI.

Returning to Corporation S meant Perry font, another

delay while Philip trained his girls to follow another set of Specs, and all spaces read as one space. The best alternative would be another Scandata bureau that read OCRB. I tried Norristown again, posing as a man with 21,000,000 characters in OCRB and no scanner to read them, and asking if they knew of any Scandata service bureaus who could do it. Including English ones. The Regional Sales Manager for the Midwest immediately came to my assistance. Yes, there were bureaus reading OCRB in Atlanta, Chicago, Columbus, Toronto, Los Angeles, Clifton (New Jersey), Springfield (Illinois), Liverpool and Wembley (England). I sent each bureau a sample of *The London Stage* as typed in Hong Kong and asked for a bid for 21,000,000 characters of the same. It was time rapidly running out, more than anything else, that caused this infidelity to ICI. I still believed that they would eventually get their scanner to read OCRB. I feared, though, that by then I'd be in England, and Will would have finished his term of employment.

Shortly after the Kansas City trip, I received a letter from Philip Hui informing me that our letter of credit had been received with thanks, except that it had been made out to China Data Systems, whereas the name in Hong Kong was Hong Kong Data Processing Company, Ltd., and the letter must agree with that name. "Thank you very much, we are only bothering about this as it becomes very important in our dealings with our bank here." I'd forgotten all about the letter of credit, because Mar Wrolstad was handling it, and I realized I'd never seen a copy of it, so I asked Mar to send over a Xerox. It read as follows.

China Data Systems Corporation
482 Hennessy Road
Hong Kong

GENTLEMEN:

We hereby establish our IRREVOCABLE IMPORT CREDIT in your favor.

For account of *Lawrence University, Appleton, Wisconsin*

By order of *First National Bank of Appleton, Appleton, Wisconsin*

not exceeding a total of US *$7,500 (Seven Thousand Five Hundred United States Dollars)*

available by your drafts at *sight* on the

FIRST WISCONSIN NATIONAL BANK OF MILWAUKEE

to be accompanied by the following documents:

Commercial Invoice and five copies, describing the merchandise as specified below.

Special Customs Invoice and one copy

Original Airway Bill of Lading, plus one non-negotiable copy, consigned to Lawrence University, c/o District Director of Customs, Milwaukee, Wisconsin, marked FREIGHT COLLECT and notify: M. O. Wrolstad, Lawrence University, Telephone: 414-739-3681.

Evidencing air shipments to Milwaukee, Wisconsin of:

PAGES OF TYPED MATERIAL FOR EDUCATIONAL INSTITUTION, PROJECT PARTIALLY SUPPORTED BY U.S. GOVERNMENT GRANT

Partial shipments are permitted. Transhipments are permitted.

Insurance is to be provided with the airline carrying the merchandise and insurance premium and freight charge will be payable at destination.

Yours very truly,
[Officers of First Wisconsin]

"Partial shipments permitted" meant, as David Shiu had explained to me, that the Milwaukee Bank would pay the Hong Kong Bank for Hong Kong Data Processing, the exact value of each shipment from Hong Kong as soon as the Milwaukee Bank was statisfied by sight of airwaybills and invoices that the goods had been delivered. I did not understand, however, why the goods were going to Milwaukee and how Mar Wrolstad entered in. Upon inquiry, I found that the bank wanted the package to come to the customs office nearest it, so that their customs broker could arrange clearance for us and transfer the documents. Mar had graciously volunteered to act for me in all this, on the assumption that I'd probably be in England when most of the shipments came. I had known that customs clearance would be required, but David Shiu had assured me that sheets of typing had no commercial value despite their cost to me, and could therefore be cleared without duty or a broker. I had visions of brokerage fees for clearing, storing, and transshipping that rivalled the cost of the merchandise itself. Furthermore, especially at first, it was necessary that the shipments pass through my hands for inspection and introduction to the scanning process. Even though I would be leaving Appleton in a few weeks, I couldn't expect Mar to do things in my place. Lastly, I had understood that I did not have to pay for any typing that was unacceptable. Not that I doubted China Data's integrity. But if nothing more than shipping documents triggered payment, it seemed to me that a box of bricks would work as well as a box of typed pages of *The London Stage*. It seemed like a classical case of being asked to buy a pig in a poke.

As I understand from previous inquiry, Air Wisconsin could clear packages from customs in Chicago and carry them to me in Appleton. If there was to be red tape, transshipment, and inspection, how could it be accomplished? No one was sufficiently concerned and informed for these tasks but me, and how could I do it with shipments going to Milwaukee and me en route to London? Most of the shipments would come after I left Appleton. Clearly, a more flexible commercial instrument must be written if that were possible.

At First Wisconsin, several people tried to help me, but at last, it was only Mr. Raul Aguilar, Director of Foreign Transactions, who seemed to know what I was talking about. He told me that I could amend the letter of credit simply by sending an order through my bank stating the amendments. I could have the goods shipped to any places I specified. I could even make personal inspection a condition of payment. However, he warned, this condition would in his view nullify the whole purpose of an irrevocable letter of credit. I did not quite understand this point, because I thought I had understood from China Data that I would have a say-so. Thereupon I took measures to have the letter of credit amended so that shipments to me at Boston, Appleton, and London were specified as alternates to Milwaukee and personal inspection preceded payment.

While the input system thus began to show cracks in its fabric, the web of fate tightened more inexorably around me. David Mann, whom I had met after Christmas at the MLA at his seminar in honor of Congreve and who had offered us the tape of his Congreve concordance, wrote to suggest a *London Stage* Information Bank seminar at next December's meeting. The fact that I would be in England did not prevent this from being a good idea in my opinion. It would allow us to develop closer relations with our clientele, to prospect for opinions and suggestions from members of the profession, and to show off our wares as proof of progress. Dean Stone, as editor of Part 4, chairman of the Advisory Board, and one-time executive secretary of the MLA, would make an excellent chairman for the seminar. I therefore passed David Mann's idea along to him. He now wrote approving the idea, and I proposed to David that some of the editors who had prepared *The*

London Stage for typing might present preliminary findings based on the printouts from our programs that I had undertaken to provide them in return for their labors. With almost six months to go before the seminar, I could certainly supply material comprehensive and accurate enough to give them something to talk about.

On Friday the 16th of July, with two more weeks left before the family's departure from Appleton for points east and the plane to London, the affairs of the *London Stage* Information Bank stood at this posture:

Editing: Leonard Leff and Muriel Friedman were done. Muriel had sent a list of O'Keefe's plays, so that I could cull the casts I'd promised her in return for her work. Leonard was sending a list of Sheridan's plays for his promised printout. Marcia Heinemann was doing her second batch and Mark Auburn his first. Batches 1, 2, 3, 4, 5, 6, and 8 had arrived in Hong Kong; 7 and 9 soon would.

Typing: When last heard from (four days ago) Philip and his girls had switched to 20 pound paper, had solved the problem of tails, and were presumably in full production. They were, however, much distressed that the name of the beneficiary on the letter of credit had not yet been changed. I hoped that the banks' slowness had not dulled their enthusiasm. If all was well, Batch 1 must be done and on the way, it being two weeks since they would have received the 20 pound paper. At their own estimated rate of typing, one week was sufficient for one batch. However, tails, paper, and the letter of credit might have hampered production.

Scanning: We would probably not know whether ICI could produce a correct magnetic tape of Hong Kong typing until the next shipment came. They had not succeeded with my homemade sample or with the test batch full of tails. This afternoon I called Lynn Courtney about it but talked to Charlie Yost instead, who assured me that everything was under control. I sent ICI an itemized list of unsolved faults and declared my need for a one-day scanning turnaround on the next shipment from Hong Kong. We would use air freight to obtain same-day delivery. My new policy with regard to ICI was to make sure that they knew precisely what I wanted in case it became necessary later on to withhold payment or break off our association, because my requirements had not been met.

Programming: Although Will had been able to find Reinhold in a Dragon at the end of April, those programs had been designed for the MT/ST sample, and they were fairly rudimentary. Since April Will had had many arduous and difficult tasks to perform in order to smooth out and speed up the programs, get them ready to handle complete batches, adjust them to the sixth edition of the Specs, the special problems of OCRB, and input by scanning. A new program, the capstone of the whole system, which made it possible to select a given datespan, set of plays, roles, or actors, or any combination of these, to produce a manageable output tailored to the scholar's need, had to be written. It was called the SELECT option of ITEMGET. Any change in one part of the system was likely to require changes everywhere else. When Will improved one routine he put others out of kilter, and there was now no way to tell whether the system was still capable of finding Reinhold but to try.

In sum, with two weeks left before I was due to leave for a year abroad, neither typing, scanning, nor programming had demonstrated adequate performance. There was no getting around the fact that by virtue of the powers and duties vested in me as director, it was my responsibility to put on a dress rehearsal of the whole system before the first of August. Typers, scanners, and the programmer were apprised of the fact, and we awaited only the arrival of the next Hong Kong shipment in order to begin the shakedown.

Monday, 19 July. Unmodified typing heads returned from China. Call D. Shiu for news: 50 pages coming. Only 50 pages? National Endowment for Humanities questions budget items in application for final phase of project. Write three-page single-spaced letter explaining. Industrial Nucleonics of Columbus calls: interested in scanning our stuff. Start assembling basic documents pertaining to input system so as to leave everyone here in possession of the important facts on editing, typing, correcting, ITEMGET search rules; input Specs, identification of batches, letters of quotation from Gerry Dowdy, David Shiu; grant rules and regulations, revised budget of 27 March; BRS itinerary; letter of credit plus amendments.

Tuesday, 20 July: Detroit Scandata Service Bureau calls. They scan Pica 72 golf ball only. Found Pica 72 golf ball on campus. Incompatible with OCRB. While home at lunch received a call from Nicholas Blacklock, manager of Computer Services Centre, Wembley, England. Can do our stuff for 5 new pence a thousand characters. Asked about SWAMI for backward *C*. He said, "SWAMI's terrible. Too slow. Our engineers can do it better by modifying the recognition circuitry. No trouble at all." Space integrity O.K. Send sample of backward *C*'s immediately. Blacklock very confident. Wrote him, "I look forward to the possibility of working with Computer Services." Said we would expect accuracy and speed in return for 25% higher cost.

Wednesday, 21 July: Gary Oakley, Computer Resources,

Toronto, called. Interested in scanning job. Wants page of backwards *C*'s from each typing head so SWAMI can learn the modification. Cabled Hong Kong to send same. Study printouts of previous ICI tests some more. Call Charlie Yost to get assurance errors can be avoided. No problem. Send list of errors to Gerry Dowdy:

1. Lines lost when they begin with equal sign. (Charles told me on the phone today that he had this licked.)
2. Spaces closed up for no apparent reason (see copy for test batch that I sent back with errors marked in red, I think with my letter of July 8. Possibly I sent it to Lynn Courtney. It was the batch we ran when I was there on 7 July).
3. *S*'s read as ampersands, possibly because of bad type, but I could see no lines crossing the *S*.
4. Asterisk at the end of line altogether lost. (Same test batch.)
5. Can you read backwards *C*? Charles says he's run this O.K.
6. What about double quote?
7. Zero reads as capital *O*. Charles says he will change it to a zero.
8. Left and right bracket read as zero.
9. Pound sign reads as zero; we want it to read as number sign.
10. Plus reads as non-printing character; we want EBCDIC code for plus. David Shiu says Hong Kong shipped us 50 pages Air Mail Monday, 19th July. Could be here Friday. Can we have turnaround of ONE DAY, please?

cc: Lynn Courtney, Charles Yost

Wrote memo detailing "Strategy for Summer" and specifications of printouts owed to Friedman, Leff, Heinemann, and Auburn. Sent this with relevant documents to Daland, Wrolstad, Dowdy, Church, Dean Stone, Yost, Shiu, Hui, Computer Center, Ruth. Asked Bob Nasternak, Lawrence 360 specialist, to take over operating programs after Will leaves. Revised Specs again to remove minor errors: seventh edition.

Thursday, 22 July: Get Mrs. Friedman's final list of O'Keefe's plays, with title variations. Keypunch same for SELECT option of ITEMGET program.

Friday, 23 July: Donnelly, Chicago and Tallman-Robbins, Springfield (Illinois), can do our scanning, Donnelly at very high price.

Saturday, 24 July: Letter from P.E.N. Blacklock, CSC. Confirms his commitment of phone call.

Sunday, 25 July: ———.

Monday, 26 July: Lawrence Computer Center calls. No chance Bob Nasternak will be able to run our leftover jobs. Too much else to do. Letter from Auburn: questions about editing. 9 p.m.: Call Philip in Hong Kong to find out how far along they are. 11 a.m. tomorrow there. They've done Batch 1 only, except for proofreading and corrections. Philip's English good. First time I ever talked to a man the soles of whose feet were facing the soles of my feet, both of us standing up. Experience cost exactly $19.95 person to person.

Tuesday, 27 July: Send Mark Batch 9 for editing. 100 sheets of typing arrive from Hong Kong (not 50?): put it on plane for Kansas City. Typing looks good. No tails. Alert ICI. "Bill Rice" will do it tomorrow. The man who actually runs the scanner?

Wednesday, 28 July: Spent morning with Will working out priorities for programming in August. Very tight because he will need about 20 days for "documentation," a sort of handbook to enable use of programs after he leaves.

Correction program for applying results of Hong Kong proofreading is no. 1.

Thursday, 29 July: Tape returns from ICI. Right bracket frequently read as left. Tape unusable. Put typing on plane again. Tell Bill to keep typing until scanning is right. Marcia has sent Batch 7 to Hong Kong.

Saturday, 31 July: Bill Rice ships second try. Air Wisconsin says TWA can't find tape in Chicago for them to bring to Appleton. Maybe Monday.

Sunday, 1 August: Depart Appleton.

Saturday's development had spoiled our chance of testing the whole type-scan-program system before we left. But I had a strategy in reserve. Our trek to Kennedy International Airport involved a week at Northport on Lake Michigan with my wife's relatives and a week in New Hampshire with mine. While the family were driving to New Hampshire from Northport, I could visit Appleton for the shakedown cruise of the *London Stage* Information Bank. I could also perhaps solve the problem of how to keep the system going after Will left, to check scanner output and fulfill our obligations to editors.

Cindy Percak. Possibly because of the rhyme, when the computer center told me that Bob Nasternak wasn't free, I thought of Cindy Percak, my advisee. Cindy had just finished her sophomore year at Lawrence. She was an English major who had accomplished a number of straight-A terms. I knew her well, because she was always changing her schedule. She spent more time than any student I've ever known collecting information about courses, in consequence of which she was always finding out good things about courses she wasn't going to take and bad things about courses she was going to take. She was constitutionally incapable of spending time unprofitably. She had a great sense of humor and a somewhat scatterbrained manner that belied her alert and essentially well-organized personality. She liked math and wanted to do some computer science. We'd talked a good bit about LSIB and I had given her computer literature to read. She wanted to do a course of independent study with me in her senior year in which she applied computer techniques to literary problems. So, on Saturday, when I decided I would go back to Appleton the following weekend, I called her at home in Deerfield, Illinois. I was triply lucky in that she was there, delighted at the prospect of operating the computer for the *London Stage* Information Bank, and free to join Will and me in Appleton on Saturday for an explanation of the work and a demonstration of the system.

Northport, at my brother and sister-in-law's isolated summer home, several miles south of the famous and exclusive compound on the Point, would have driven computers out of my mind if any place could have. Besides the cheerful company of my unbelievably good and good-natured mother-in-law, named Dear Boo; our gracious Aunty Lyn; and Kay's other brother's wife, Janet, and her two boys, Chris and Michael; and all of us Schneiders except Devon who was working in Boston, we had the distraction of the *Alacrity*, an English fiberglass and teakwood cruising sloop just big enough to sleep two. It was graceful, sturdy, and convenient without any fuss. I spent the week under cloudless skies carried along in the *Alacrity* by fresh breezes or sitting on the smooth crescent of sandy beach from which the other side of the bay was dimly visible across sparking blue water. Every chance I got I took people for sailboat rides though I must admit that once or twice I was the only one that wanted to go. Against this background my computer business clashed violently. No wonder that Lyn voiced the misgiving about English teachers computing that eventually started this book. Not only daily calls back and forth to Appleton and to Kansas

City and New York, but constant worry about what was going on there absented my mind from its proper response to my body's setting.

On Tuesday I discovered that the tape it had taken us four Kansas City flights to obtain was unusable because the zeroes were still unaccountably being read as capital *O*'s. After stewing over this for a day, I called Lynn Court-ney in Kansas City and asked him what ICI was willing to do about this state of affairs. Would they, for instance, pay all costs for shipping unusable tapes to Appleton, guarantee one day's turnaround at ICI, and pay damages to us for all delays beyond this that were their fault? Lynn said, after absorbing this blast, "You sound like a man who is looking for someone else to do his business." He could have meant: 1) "I don't want your business," 2) "If you want this kind of service you'll have to look elsewhere," or just possibly he meant literally 3) "You seem to be looking for someone else to do your business," which was true. At any rate, by now I think he knew I knew that I could refuse to pay for inadequate goods, but I don't think he knew that his words were so close to the truth. "Ben," he continued, while I pondered his canny remark, "we can pay for transportation of bad tapes, but I can't promise the rest of those things. All I can say is we will bust our ass to get these tapes to you and that's the best anybody can do. We want your business."

In Appleton on the weekend of August 7th and 8th Cindy vindicated my choice of her by catching on astonish-ingly fast to the intricacies of the *London Stage* system stored in GWSJR1 and the operating system of the 360. Will's method of teaching a person to run the computer was to assign his pupil a task and see what hapened. Having had the benefit of this tutelage once or twice myself, I could well appreciate the speed with which Cindy assimilated the complicated steps required to get a program running. In no time, she could activate the computer, mount tapes and disks, punch parameter cards, write commands on the console typewriter, start up the printer and the card reader, and read the main signal lights. In short, she managed better after one afternoon than I did after one year. Indeed, the sight of Will and Cindy grooving together so effortlessly with the 360 brought home the fact that computing is a youthful métier, foreign only to those who matured before computers.

The second hundred pages from Hong Kong, though improperly scanned, were sufficiently correct to demonstrate the functioning of the current versions of ICIFIX, ICISCAN (formerly SAVEDT), STRUCTUR, LADDER, ITEMGET (with SELECT) and SORTMERGE, but unhappily we couldn't get much past ICIFIX before Cindy had to go back to Deerfield. We assured her and ourselves that Will's documentation, my July 21st "Strategy for the Summer," and today's discussion would enable her to carry on in the fall. On Sunday, after her departure, this sub-batch of Batch 1 passed through ICISCAN, STRUCTUR, LADDER, and ITEMGET with the greatest of ease, but our attempts at sorting of ITEMGET output "bombed," and we didn't get a chance to run the SELECT option. Will was not visibly perturbed by either development.

However, on Monday, August 9th, as I prepared to leave Appleton the second time, to join my family in New Hampshire, none of our programs had been tested on a full batch of *The London Stage,* and SORTMERGE had failed on a fraction of Batch 1. Cindy had seen no demonstration of most of the programs. ICI had not scanned any typing acceptably. The rest of Batch 1 had not yet come from China. They would now have to type at the rate of

2200 pages per week to finish by the 31st of August. With this lagging schedule, scanning in London began to seem more and more attractive.

Shifting to London would undoubtedly introduce new incompatibilities for Will and Cindy to deal with. I decided to call P.E.N. Blacklock at CSC and try to get some advance notice of what might go wrong. In a letter, I had already listed 15 possible problems that I knew of from working with Compuscan, Corporation S, and ICI. Now I wanted to hear what Nick Blacklock would say about each in turn. At 10 a.m. his time, 5 a.m. mine, I got through. CSC, it was most apparent, had given thought to our job and Nick could talk about specific measures for dealing with each of the 15 points. One great advantage of CSC's service was that they had a computer as well as a scanner and could supply me with printouts of scanner output. By checking printouts, I could prevent disastrous episodes like ICI's airfreighting us two bad tapes of the same hundred pages at $18.85 per flight. It was also an advantage that Wembley and my London flat were close to terminals of London Transport.

Despite Lynn Courtney's assurances, there was still the question of whether ICI *could* do what they *would* do. A shift to London would almost certainly introduce complications and delays. There was enough money in the project budget to extend Will's appointment another ten days, to the 10th of September—time enough, I thought, for CSC to scan Batch 2, and for Will to test the product before he left. Will's tasks would be to improve the documentation, which by nature could always stand improvement, and run off the printouts of Sheridan's plays for Leonard Leff and of O'Keefe's plays for Muriel Friedman. The process would provide the shakedown of the *London Stage* Information Bank that I thought must take place while Will was still around to remove any last-minute bugs. I called David

Shiu in New York and told him to have Hong Kong send Batch 2 to me in London, but to send Batch 1 directly to Kansas City, bypassing Appleton. There still might be time before I left the country for Will to test the system on a full batch. Batch 1 would also provide Muriel with one-third of her data and Leonard one-fourth of his. This double course, I realized, was dangerous, because if Lynn discovered that I was being faithless, ICI certainly would not damage its posterior for the *London Stage* Information Bank and Batch 1 might wither on the vine. I gambled that he wouldn't give an English professor credit for having the sense to shop around.

In New Hampshire there was very little of the lolling about on a sailboat kind of thing because this was our last chance to show my son Ben some eastern colleges before he went off to do his senior year of high school in England. Staying awake on the freeways was our chief diversion during that last week. On Friday word came via David Shiu in New York that Batch 1 was crossing the Pacific and I called Bill Rice (I think from the Arrow Shirt factory store in Waterville, Maine) to make clear how lovely it would be if a tape of this data reached Will in time for him to try out the tape and our programs before I left the States at midnight next Wednesday. He said he'd be glad to do the scanning, even on Saturday, if the typing came. Batch 1 did arrive in Kansas City on Saturday, but U. S. Customs encouraged Bill to think that he could not clear it from customs without a broker. That meant that nothing could be done until Monday. The broker consumed Monday (I imagine) pretending to wrestle with red tape to justify his exorbitant fee. That was that. I told Bill to mail the tape to Will when he got around to it. I would fly to London not knowing whether 15 months of work had produced a functioning *London Stage* Information Bank or not.

Nor were U.S. Customs the only unexpected last-minute complication. David Shiu had invited us all to have dinner for him on our next-to-last evening before emplaning. Victor Fung, President of China Data, was to join us. We duly met, not far from our hotel, at a quiet, dimly lit, luxuriously appointed Chinese Restaurant called The Lotus, in great expectation of having the best-ever in a long series of best-ever Chinese meals. Victor and David greeted us with warmth and dignity and led us to a round table set for six. (Devon was still working in Boston and Ben was driving the car back to New Hampshire.) Both Victor and David were startlingly younger than I had expected. The President, if anything, looked even younger than the Vice-President of Sales. Both could have been under 30. It developed that they had just come from their offices at the First National City Bank of New York, and they dressed the part. Their being primarily international bankers explained to me why China Data often seemed a bit ephemeral. But as the sideline of international bankers it also had enough solidity to rescue it from the Viatron category.

The meal which our hosts chose for us after earnest discussion of the menu in Chinese was no disappointment. As we sat back happily over coffee David informed us with apologies that Victor had some business to discuss. "You must remove the personal approval clause from the letter of credit," he said matter-of-factly. "I thought it was all right," I said looking at David, who looked down. "No, it nullifies the whole point of the letter of credit," Victor explained—echoing Raul Aguilar. I timidly wondered what guarantee there was, then, that the goods were as ordered when paid for. "The fact that we must supply good merchandise to stay in business," he replied. "If there is anything wrong we'll be glad to correct it." Nevertheless, I thought, I did not pay ICI or my grocer until I had seen the goods, and although I promised Victor to execute an amendment the following day that struck out the personal approval clause, and although we parted cheerfully, having been royally feasted, I was at a loss to understand what seemed a sudden change of policy, and I wondered if it betokened a change in China Data's attitude toward our custom.

Much later that evening with some relief it came to me why in this case I had to pay for my goods without looking at them. An exporter simply couldn't afford to operate on any other terms. Imagine how helpless you would be with ten thousand pounds of tea sitting on a dock in a foreign land. What guarantee would you have that your customer would not, due to a sudden change in the tea market, decide your tea wasn't any good and refuse to pay? Could you have it shipped back for nothing? Could you sell it to someone else at the agreed-on price? Your position would clearly be intolerable and untenable; hence, you require a letter of credit that is irrevocable. The importer must take the risk or there can be no transaction whatsoever. Victor's firmness in this matter did not represent a change in attitude, then; it was simply an assertion of the usual policy.

CHAPTER VII
OF OUTPUT

The Author visits CSC in Wembley & discovers a little-known Railway Line. The Crises of 10th and 30th September, and of 15th October, including a narrow view of IBM-London, the reason for Hong Kong's Delay, a lecture on Communications, the Initial Punctuation Disaster, & the Author's battle with BOAC & H.M. Customs. The Crisis of 11th December, in which the Author exports and imports the same shipment, & learns an expensive lesson in Capitalization.

Two days after we landed in London I visited Computer Services Centre. I learned more about London Transport in getting from our flat in NW1 to their premises in Wembley than I'd learned in a year on my previous sabbatical. I soon saw that the half-hour I had allowed for the trip was not enough. The line from Camden Town, where I lived, to Stonebridge Park, where Nick had told me to get off, looked much straighter on the elegant London Transport map than the route actually taken by the train. It looked as if all I had to do was ride down the black Northern Line to King's Cross, change to the yellow Circle Line and ride across to Paddington, then change to the brown Bakerloo Line for a northwest slant over to Stonebridge Park. The map did not show that I would walk a quarter of a mile between the stations where I changed, and I had not realized that all the little studs signified station stops, nor had I realized that at Queen's Park on the slanted part it would be all change for British Rail and a good wait until British Rail happened along with its quaint eight-seater compartments all slashed in ruins by soccer enthusiasts. At Stonebridge Park, now high above street level instead of underground, the train stopped for ten seconds, nine of which I spent struggling to open the compartment door. I finally burst onto the platform as the train rolled off laughing.

Computer Services Centre occupied the second and third (third and fourth) floors of a giant concrete and aluminum office building on stilts which also housed some of Lever Brothers, London Weekend television, and a score of smaller fry. This building, just for fun, was oval in cross section rather than rectangular, and it surveyed a vast wasteland consisting of railroad yards, a torn-up road intersection, streams of traffic, and dingy shops, with Wembley Stadium far in the distance. Aesthetically it could not begin to explain what it was doing there, but practically it was fifty yards from Stonebridge Park Station and fifty yards from the intersection of North Circular Road and Harrow Road (which anyone who has not tried to drive there might consider an advantage). Although it had to have been there for a year at least, its bare unplanted grounds were littered with builders' debris, piles of dirt, shreds of paper blown about like autumn leaves, and rusting metal. A perfect set for an Italian movie. Inside, the English, who with some justice detest everything new and mass produced, were doing their best to take the shine off of it. Walls had been smudged, wall-to-wall carpets stained, fixtures pulled off, windows filmed, furniture broken and bedusted, doors kicked into submission and corners converted to warehouses. After only a year or so, it was nearly livable.

On the third (fourth) floor, P.E.N. Blacklock, protected by a receptionist and a secretary, reigned in considerable contemporary grandeur at a large desk in a large room, wearing a dark blue pin-striped suit with a vest, and a tie with emblems on it which was neither wide nor narrow. He was, I could see, ten or twenty years my junior. It developed that he held an Oxford degree in psychology, lived eighty miles north, near Cambridge, in a Georgian country house, and drove there for weekends in an Alfa Romeo. The toughness I'd felt on the phone did not now enter in. Now it was Nick and Ben, please and thank you, and not at all and after you, and won't you have a cup of coffee or a cup of tea. He pressed buttons, summoning Barry Layfield, a youthful but substantial director of development, for a reassuring discussion of the fifteen points. Barry made me want to write a book named *Tom Swift and His Computing Machine.* We went to see the scanner and successfully ran off some pages of OCRB typing that I had brought with me. There we met the scanner's boss, a cheerful lad named Roger Williams, who did not know that a man by that name had founded Rhode Island, and the chief programmer, Martin Best, who did know he was not related to George Best of Manchester United although he was good-looking enough to qualify. Then we parted, to await the arrival of Batch 2.

On the trip back I brought to light little-known features of London Transport. When the inbound train stopped at Stonebridge Park I scrambled into the nearest compartment and sat down. For a while I couldn't imagine why the two ladies in there with me giggled and looked at me and why at the next stop a lady who got on looked offended and a gent who started to climb in changed his

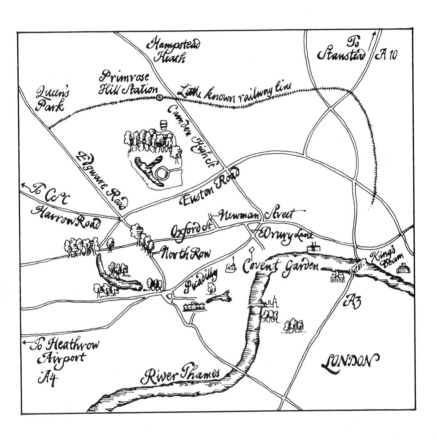

mind in terror. Then I deciphered the backwards sign on the glass door: "Ladies Only." The ladies, seeing I'd caught on and didn't mean to intrude, protested that it was perfectly all right. But after a few strained runs I changed at a station to an unsegregated amenity. In my new setting there was a map of the railway line. It claimed to be heading for Primrose Hill, which I knew to be only a few blocks from our flat. By finding this lost railway line I cut the travel time from my flat to CSC in half.

On Monday, the 23rd of August, Computer Services Centre was ready to start as soon as Batch 2 arrived. Batch 2 should now be on its way, because David had said at dinner in New York on the 14th that it was almost finished. ICI might or might not have scanned Batch 1; Will might or might not have run Muriel's and Leonard's tabulations, giving the system the rigorous test it had to have before he left.

Tuesday, 24 August: Cable Philip Hui to ship Batch 2 to London, in case he hasn't got the word from Philip. Send samples of first 100 pages to Nick. Study 8 August printouts of second 100 pages. Girls have curious unexplainable habit of putting $ sign after typist's page number every once in a while. Habit left over from earlier job? Write Philip to have them stop.

Wednesday, 25 August: Write Will asking if Batch 1 is scanned and in hand.

Thursday, 26 August: Victor Fung writes, "Please be assured that every aspect of the job will be in order." Find out from August 8th printouts that LADDER sometimes fails to produce casts when an update is involved. Report to Will.

Friday, 27 August: Bought ten 2400-foot tapes from Minnesota Mining (London) for the ten batches CSC will scan. Check printouts of August 8th.

Monday, 30 August: Amend July 21st "Strategy for Summer" to accommodate scanning in London, giving top priority to batches required for editors' printouts.

Tuesday, 31 August: Write Ruth Lesselyong, faculty secretary, ask her to find out from Will if Batch 1 is scanned and safely in hand, tell me. If Hong Kong is to finish by August 31st they will have to send 6500 pages today.

Wednesday, 1 September: Investigate H.M. Customs regulations bearing on typing from Hong Kong. After seven phone calls find out that visit (with sample) to King's Beam House near Tower is recommended action. At Enquiries Desk there am assured that what I have is typing, that typing is not dutiable, that its code category is 4906017, and that the appropriate clearance form is C.11, which I can fill out by myself without the aid of any customs broker whatever. Did not see any King's Beam: "Public standard [scale] formerly in custody of Grocers' Company"—Oxford English Dictionary. Write Philip expressing great distress over slowness of Batch 2, curious $ signs after typists' page numbers.

Thursday, 2 September: At last. Receive printouts of Batch 1 from Will. Note from him says we should stick with ICI because quality is now high. Says he's not going back to school as planned, after all (available). Has written program routine to take care of curious dollar signs. "Apparently China Data thinks $ is necessary when a space is associated with the typist's entry." Check Specs. "Each line must contain exactly 75 characters. . . . When a space would be the 76th character begin the next line with an @. . . . If the next line falls on a new page, this extra space follows the typist's initial, page number, and space: 'D31#@'." Hah. Custom of using # to signify a blank apparently unknown in China. Since no # available on OCRB typing element, they used the closest thing: $! Make date for phone call to Will at IPC computer, 1 a.m., 9 September, the day before he leaves. 6 a.m. here.

Friday, 3 September: Visit Roy Wisbey at Literary Computing Centre, Cambridge. University furnishes them three paper tape punches with typewriter keyboards, girls to punch text, their own room. First special provisions for literary computing I've heard of. Punt on Cam with wife, children, friends, relatives; three punts, great chaos.

Saturday, 4 September: This is ridiculous. Write Philip, Victor, and David asking them to explain why Batch 2 isn't here.

Sunday, 5 September: Proofread Will's printout of Batch 1. Not as good as he thought. Scanner reads *p* and *g* as *P* and 9, left parenthesis as left bracket. These are new mistakes. Capital *O* now reads as capital *O* and zero reads as zero. They could if they would.

Monday, 6 September: Word from bank that approval clause has been taken out of letter of credit. Mark Auburn has mailed Batch 9 to Hong Kong.

Tuesday, 7 September: Cable David Shiu to please explain why I don't have Batch 2. Write Gerry Dowdy about *P,* 9, and left paren. Receive cable from Philip announcing imminent arrival of Batch 2 on BOAC 807.

Wednesday, 8 September: BOAC says 807 arrives this afternoon. Call BOAC freight around 6. Package not on hand yet. Receive research proposal from Leonard Leff for Folger's Shakespeare Library Fellowship, seeking my recommendation. Proposal most interesting: "It seems likely that nagging questions about sentimentality as well as the denigration of the Irish in *The Rivals* could be answered by reviewing the careers of actors who played controversial roles." Precisely. Wrote Leonard that if he wants to find out why Sheridan cast the play as he did, he should study all the other roles of the actors Sheridan picked, instead of the casts of all performances of Sheridan's plays, as planned. Wrote David Mann my conviction that Leff's research would make excellent example of how *London Stage* Information Bank can help theatre history. Assured him that both Leonard and Muriel would have printouts with which to illustrate their remarks in plenty of time for seminar.

Thursday, 9 September: 5 a.m. Will doesn't answer when I call computer as prearranged. 8 a.m. Package is on hand at BOAC. Tell them I will clear it myself. Drive to air-port. Find cargo village. BOAC not there. Find BOAC. Package already cleared, "entry preparation" £3.25 ($8). Drop goods at CSC. Inside the package was a neat long-hand message on Hong Kong Data Processing stationery: "Dear Prof. Ben. Very sorry to have to write you this way, anyway. I just want to give a brief explanation on this shipment. The enclosed information sheet will explain everything. The sequence for the Batch numbers should be according to the information sheet."

And that was that. On the 9th of September the third attempt to run a full test of LSIB before Will left had fizzled. With Batch 9 done, only two batches (10, 11) re-mained to be edited. Only two batches had been typed. At the present rate of typing eleven batches would take a year. One batch had been scanned, imperfectly. It would have to do unless scanning with CSC proved infeasible and we completed the job with ICI. At least Will's last set of print-outs had included a successful output of the final program that had bombed on August 8th and the new printout demonstrated that ICISCAN, STRUCTUR, and LAD-DER worked on the full Batch 1. But I had no evidence that we could produce Muriel's and Leonard's compilations, as promised. When I did get through to him on the 10th, Will said he was free to stay on for a while, and because he had taken a Christmas vacation there did happen to be enough money in the salary budget. It also turned out that documentation and debugging had taken up so much of his time he hadn't finished ICIFRONT, the program for automatically applying correction instructions from Hong Kong's proofreading to the text. I proposed that he finish out the month of September to process forthcoming Batch 2 tapes and finish ICIFRONT. "I wouldn't mind doing that," he said. Now we had twenty days in which to accomplish a reading of Batch 2 at CSC and verify it on our system.

Twenty days, however, were not enough. When you are dealing with limited liability companies, all of which observe weekends religiously, twenty days are actually only fourteen days. And when time must be allowed for shipping and customs clearance, as few as seven days may be included in twenty. Add to this that two companies must combine to produce the final product, each having a shipping and receiving ritual, requiring as much as a day, and only six days are left. This leaves hardly any margin for error in a very error-prone business.

CSC used their share of the time very efficiently. Batch 2 arrived on Friday afternoon. On Monday afternoon I received a printout of the first part with a note from Nick warning that "We have not had a chance to check this completely." If they had, they would have noted that *p*'s read as *P*'s, *y*'s read as *Y*'s, *O*'s read as zeroes, and periods (known in England as full stops) were missed entirely when they fell at the beginning of lines as a result of our policy of breaking every line arbitrarily after the 75th character. Upon hearing of this, Nick instantly called into action the whole programming and engineering power of Interscan Data, the international branch of Scandata, housed on the same floor in the same building as CSC. They in turn cabled the head office in the United States for the technique of reading periods at the beginning of lines, and on the second day they had the method installed and working on samples from their typewriter. On the third and fourth day they ran off the first part of 2 again, but they still had trouble with full stops, *y*, and *p*. On the fifth day they achieved a nearly errorless reading of the first part of 2 and we determined to send it.

At this point a new company unexpectedly entered into the picture. CSC's computer used the ASCII or American Standard Code for Information Interchange. And our computer in Appleton used IBM's private code called EBCDIC (Extended Binary Coded Decimal Interchange Code). Only a computer that possesses tape decks mechanically compatible with both kinds of tape can translate ASCII to EBCDIC. So it was CSC's custom, when "IBM-compatible" tapes were required, to have their ASCII tapes converted to EBCDIC at IBM's data processing service on Newman Street (near the Post Office Tower). In order to accommodate outside jobs, IBM had a staff of customer's agents who interfaced the jobs to the giant 370 machine at Newman Street. These agents worked at another IBM office in North Row about two miles southwest of Newman Street near Marble Arch, gaining access to the 370 at Newman Street by means of a terminal.

For jobs like ours, you deposited the input tape and a blank one for output in the tape library at Newman Street, told the librarian the identifying names of the tapes and relayed the same information to your agent at North Row. He then put on the program at North Row and the librarian passed your tapes to the Newman Street computer operator when the machine asked for them. Then, when the job was done, the agent in due course found out the result and told you or didn't find out the result and didn't tell you or found out the result and didn't tell you. It he didn't tell you, you could find out by calling him, if he wasn't out to lunch or on vacation, or didn't know. If he was out to lunch or on vacation, you could usually get someone else in his department to rummage around on his desk for the information. If you couldn't find out this way, and if you had the job number, you could call Newman Street (but better to go in person) and enquire its status. You had to get the job number from North Row when you deposited the tapes at Newman Street. If you had the job number, and the job was done, the tape librarian would give you the computer's report on the job. If you knew how to read that, you could tell how many blocks (units of data) had been converted, and if you knew how many blocks the original tape contained you could tell whether the run had been successful. If the agent was out to lunch or on vacation and his colleague could not find the information on his desk and you did not know the job number or if you couldn't decipher the job report or did not know how many blocks the original tape contained you had no way of finding out whether the program had worked. Even if it had worked you wouldn't know for sure until the tape had been copied and printed on paper in Appleton.

In spite of IBM the tape was converted on the sixth day, and on the evening of the sixth day I put the product on Seaboard Flight 605 leaving early the next morning for Chicago. There on the same day Air Wisconsin was to clear it from customs and carry it to Will, or at least so I had directed on the airwaybill. Not so. First it was lost in Chicago. Then it was found and sent via North Central Airlines to Green Bay thirty miles north of Appleton, where on some days a U.S. Customs agent drops in. On the 30th of September this customs agent and Will went to Green Bay and the agent handed over CSC's tape of Batch 2, Part 1, but the tape was useless. It had the wrong EBCDIC code for brackets, the colon, the dollar, the plus and equal signs, the question and exclamation marks, and the space. I therefore asked Will to stay on until October 15th. If necessary I would rob Peter to pay Paul, reducing the amount of data typed in Hong Kong to free funds for Will's salary, but an extrapolation of the cost of Batches 1 and 2 made it evident that I had for once budgeted more than I needed for an item and could afford Will one more half-month period.

The advent of the weekly two-day vacation of the 2nd of October prevented any action on the faulty conversion until Monday the 4th. CSC's own tape, it was discovered, used codes for the dollar, plus and equals signs, question and exclamation marks, colons, brackets, and spaces that IBM's programs did not recognize. By the 7th of October, this incompatibility had been adjusted and I *mailed* the tape to Appleton (to avoid the racketeers of Chicago and Green Bay). On the 15th I called Will. The tape was there and it was good. I thanked him for his great contribution to the project and bade him farewell. Then I wrote Cindy a letter about the heavy responsibilities that now rested on her shoulders, emphasizing the overdue printouts for Leonard and Muriel.

The events of the next months are blurs in a choking smog of restless anxiety. Inexorably plans for the seminar at MLA took shape. Dean Stone's application to the organizers of the convention was accepted. He sent announcements of it to interested journals, which were in due course published. David Mann duly invited Muriel Friedman and Leonard Leff to talk about their LSIB-assisted research and they gladly accepted. And I had already promised them tailor-made compilations of actor-role data as a basis for their papers, well in advance. Lewis Sawin's advice, "Get results," still rang in my ears, and, heeding Will's wise words, "You never know whether it will work until you try it out," I was fiercely determined that the seminar must be our total system's final proving ground. But when David Mann announced his program, little more than a month before the seminar, neither Muriel nor Leonard had their printouts.

During these months no telephone or doorbell rang that did not produce a flash of hope that it heralded good news from China, CSC, or Cindy. It hardly ever did. In my determination I continually brushed aside the force of Murphy's Law, being by each day's unbelievable events more and more convinced that everything that could happen had already happened. I did not stop to think in how many points the *London Stage* system was vulnerable to accident. I did not reckon with the possibilities for error in the Scandata 300, IBM Newman Street, artificial communication (defined as any communication that is not face to face), and self-generated information (defined as whatever you believe that you haven't seen). I committed what Alfred North Whitehead has called "the fallacy of misplaced concreteness" in my faith that these systems were independent entities actually performing the functions that by definition they are said so perform. For example, I believed that what I meant to say in a letter was what I did say. I had faith that what I intended had been expressed, that what was expressed had been delivered, and that what had been delivered had been understood and acted upon and that by then the time for action hadn't passed. Actually, a letter is not a thing; the idea of a deity has more concreteness than this idea. I was also to learn among other things that the idea of a Scandata 300 is not a Scandata 300, that the idea

of BOAC is not BOAC, and that the idea of IBM Newman Street is not IBM Newman Street.

The true cause of Hong Kong Data Processing's slowness illustrates the insubstantiality of messages and the
danger of self-generated information. My frantic cables in
September to New York and Hong Kong asking why
Batch 2 was so long in coming produced an explanation
from Victor which I received on the 20th of September.
The requirement that every line must have 75 characters
in it meant that the work could not be divided into arbitrary
units so that typists who had finished could share the load of
typists who hadn't. Philip had interpreted my specification
of "75 characters in every line, 30 lines on every page" in
the strictest sense, to mean that every page except the last
had to be full to the 75th character of the last line. This
could be accomplished only if one typist did a whole
batch by herself, of if a series of typists worked one after
another. If several worked in parallel, simultaneously, there
was no chance that the last page of each girl's typing would
be full to the 75th character of the 30th line. Fortunately,
Philip did decide to parcel out the work in theatrical seasons, as the text does, one season per girl, allowing an incomplete last page for each season. But there was still no
way for girls who finished short seasons to join girls with
long seasons. This interpretation of the Specs worked an
even greater hardship in the typing of correction instructions, because these had to be correct as they stood. If they
made an error in these that contracted or expanded the text,
the only way to avoid incomplete pages was to retype
everything from the error onwards over again. Corrections
for one batch could be 30 pages long. Nor was there any
way of dividing up the load for corrections.

Both Philip and I were operating on self-generated
information: he assuming that I meant my full-page rule
in the strictest sense and I assuming that my artificial communication achieved my intention. If either Philip or I had

for an instant suspected the truth we would have acted immediately to remove the difficulty. I only meant to get as much scanning for my money as I could. I didn't mean for them to slow down to increase characters per page. I immediately wrote Philip to ignore the full-page rule, but by this time, they'd been typing for four and one-half months. His girls had already typed well into Batch 6. The moral of *Howard's End* has practical as well as social application. "Only connect."

After September the rate of typing on the 21st floor of the Thai Kong Building doubled, but it didn't speed up quite enough to allow for a comfortable margin of time before 1) Cindy Percak went home for Christmas vacation and 2) Leonard Leff and Muriel Friedman gave their talks at the MLA convention between Christmas and New Year's. Because scanning and other things took longer than expected, Cindy did not have the batches from which Muriel's printout were to be taken until the middle of November and she didn't even get the last of Leonard's batches until the 13th of December. The reason for this was that in response to my urging, as recorded in my entry for the 8th of September, Leonard now required data from Batch 9 as well as 6 and 1, in order to get the early careers of actors in Sheridan's plays. Since Marcia Heinemann and Mark Auburn had not yet defined their needs I was free to rearrange priorities, and on the 15th of October I cabled Philip to do Batch 9 immediately after Batch 6. We didn't actually need Batches 4 and 5 right away, but they were already done. Furthermore, the girls had already finished Batch 7 and had started on Batch 8, neither of which was important from the new frame of reference established on the 8th of September. Actually I had committed the fallacy of misplaced concreteness again. I had gotten so used to the batch numbers I had assigned to the volumes in July that I believed the only way one could get to Batch 9 was

to do Batches 1, 2, 3, 4, 5, 6, 7, 8, and I had been devoting full energy to this futile goal.

BOAC easily shattered my idea of an airline. At about
midnight on the 11th of October, armed with letters from
H.M. Customs, I asserted my right to collect Batch 3 at
BOAC Cargo in Heathrow Airport, where I happened
truly to be when the shipment came in, without paying
£3.25 for customs clearance entry preparation. After pondering these documents some minutes and showing them
around, Mrs. M. R. Eldridge, cargo clerk to BOAC, said
I could clear these myself only by taking my entry to the
Long Room. This, I found, was in a barracks-like building
about a mile away. True to the British style of nomenclature
it was no more long than New College Oxford is new.
There I was told to come back at 8 a.m. Upon my fruitless
return to the freight desk Mrs. Eldridge very kindly took
me upstairs into a vast complex of cubicles, desks, business
machines, and CRT terminals, to find the Customs Officer
on night duty. He was away, but he came back after a
while. The real problem was—there is a beautiful irony
in this that I cannot enjoy—that BOAC had just computerized the whole process of customs clearance. In England
airlines act as their customers' customs broker. As I understand it the computer system made no provision for clearance outside of LACES (London Airport Cargo Electronic
data processing Scheme). LACES, besides keeping all
the freight and duty straight, performed the function of randomly selecting shipments for inspection by a customs
officer. The only way to find out whether a given shipment
was selected was to prepare a LACES clearance entry and
key the data into a CRT terminal. In a second or two the
screen would say, if it didn't choose the shipment for inspection, "Airwaybill 061-0343-6602 cleared for entry."
It also gave the weight and charges in the currency of the
airwaybill. On command it would convert this to pounds

at the going rate. It would do everything but accommodate personal feeless entry preparation. On this particular night I somehow persuaded BOAC that even if they did make out an entry I shouldn't be charged. I said that although Batch 3 cost U.S. $812.40 as on the airbill, it had no commercial value. It was as useless as waste paper to any-one but me. The customs officer agreed and told the clerk to treat the shipment as personal effects. I did get stuck, however, with a larger than normal handling charge. I guess I had required unusual handling.

Batches 4 and 5 never got to Heathrow, but landed 40 miles north at a place called Stanstead, because freight handlers at Heathrow were having a wildcat strike. It only took a day to find out what had happened to the plane and whether the shipment had arrived on it. At Stanstead every-thing was very informal. The agent helped me fill out my own entry, spending almost as much time on it as it would have taken to do it himself. After we had completed the formalities, he said it might take half an hour to find the package and bring it over to the office, so I decided to have a cup of tea with my wife in the airport restaurant and then go back for the package. After about fifteen minutes he appeared in the restaurant bearing the package. For all these kindnesses there was not even a handling charge.

The scanner at CSC did not behave at all like the idea of a Scandata scanner. To enumerate in detail all the other things it did besides read the pages of *The London Stage* fed into it, would take almost as many pages as I have now written. It was more like a human being than a machine. It had good days and bad days and when you got it so it would do one thing right, it started doing another wrong. My faith that once the Scandata engineers had got it to pro-duce correct text, it would continue to do so, was un-founded. Although it was working well on Batches 2 and 3 by the end of October it was totally incapable of reading Batches 4 and 5 during the month of November. It made all kinds of mistakes of the sort I have noted already, but principally it refused to read the full stop at the beginning of a line. One morning after 4 and 5 had been fully and unacceptably processed for the third time, I went to Nick's office to remonstrate. His response was to call the President of Interscan Data, put him on the intercom and have me tell my story, as if to say to me, "Here is the responsible party." The voice on the intercom replied almost exactly like this: "Nick, I have told you this before and I will tell you again: this machine was not designed to read a full stop at the beginning of a line. It never has and never will read a full stop at the beginning of a line." It was true that the scanner had missed more than a few initial full stops in Batches 2 and 3, but initial full stops were rare and the aggregate number of errors per 100,000 characters was acceptable. But it was missing all the initial full stops in Batches 4 and 5, and sometimes commas and colons too.

Nick decided that since the girls in his typing pool weren't busy at present he'd have them mark all the punctuation at the beginning of a line so that the scanner would fail to recognize the mark, stop, and flash it on the screen. Then the operator could see what was supposed to be there and put it in by hand from the control typewriter. This might have worked if there had been an established way of making the marks. But this was an entirely new technique. Various kinds of marks were made in various places by various people and the result was total disaster, possibly even irreparable. Sometimes the scanner operator couldn't tell what mark of punctuation was intended and he put in the wrong one. Sometimes he couldn't see how much space followed and he put in the wrong space. Sometimes he could see, but he couldn't get the machine to execute the right space because of the position and shape of the mark. Sometimes the machine read the mark as an erroneous character without stopping! The marks could not be removed without making the problem worse.

I offer this account not as an example of corporate inefficiency, unless by Scandata, but as one example of what lengths CSC was willing to go to to meet its commitment to a customer whose copy was prepared under circumstances beyond their control in a style they would never have recommended. I hate to think how many hours were wasted on Batches 4 and 5, but when I offered to accept faulty readings at half price, to end these repeated failures, and Nick's people leapt at the chance, he told them they must do the job right and give me what CSC had promised. As to what CSC had promised, there was never even so much as a handshake (unless social) between us or a letter from him to specify exactly what he would do for 5 new pence a thousand. Perhaps this was dangerous, but when I took in the public school-Oxford background and read the unstated meaning of his words, I thought the best and pleasantest policy was to depend on his word as a gentleman. Best policy, because a gentleman will do more for you than you could ever write into a contract and pleasantest because trust removes distrust, suspicion, and worry. I was not disappointed.

The public school tradition had other effects on business. If you wrote Nick a letter, you would get an answer the next day. If you left word for him to call, the response was not so automatic. This state of affairs is the reverse of American business custom as I experienced it, where, like as not, if the matter doesn't warrant the expense of a phone call you'll never get a letter about it. If it does warrant a call, your chances of hearing more are better. But the surest way (if he's in) is to call him yourself.

British business, if CSC is an example, also moves at a more gentle and considerate pace than American. I had a good chance to observe it because, to speed things up and meet my American deadline, I spent many hours at CSC proofreading scanner output. I didn't see any malingering at the water cooler, but I did observe some leisurely business conferences around this or that desk. I think it was business. I could also tell that there was a lightly organized social life running parallel to business, filling lunch hours and weekends with sports and games and get-togethers, indoors and outdoors, both segregated as to sex and integrated. Management must certainly have favored these morale-building doings, but I could see no evidence of management's cold organizing hand. I heard once of a young woman who wouldn't change to a better-paying job because the games were so good where she was.

I was invited several times to have lunch in the board-room. Entertaining customers was the apparent function of these luncheons. The manager of the typing pool, a gracious lady, became hostess on these occasions and the ranking company officer was host; that is, he passed out the before-dinner sherry. Junior secretaries set the table, "dished up," and disappeared. I think the meals came out of a big hot metal case of the sort lifted onto airliners, but it was of course served from proper dishes, not trays. After a leisurely glass of sherry, with nuts, came soup, chop or cutlet, two vegetables, roast potato, green salad, a sweet with double cream, cheese and biscuits, and coffee, the whole accompanied by a good bottle or two of claret. Conversation was general and shop was not talked. It is said that in Britain there is a cult of the car. It is true.

I concluded that the British style tries to make business seem as much like pleasure as possible, while not neglecting it. The American style, on the other hand, in which business is strictly business, may have the disadvantage of encouraging people to seek their pleasure elsewhere, and thence to avoid business whenever they can get away with it. The whole spirit of British office life is summed up for me in a series of billboard ads that show a participant in the midst of a vigorous rowing or rugby match holding aloft a pint of beer. The caption reads, "I'm only here for the beer." The lad is saying, really, that games are a social activity and so, truly, is business, although it is not a game.

———————

About the middle of November, when I realized that Batches 4 and 5, not needed for the seminar, had, thanks to undecipherable markings, become a unique problem the solution of which would not contribute to the progress of any future batches, I asked Nick to set them aside and concentrate all efforts on scanning Batches 6 and 9 as soon as possible after they arrived, because they were needed for our demonstration at the convention and had to be processed in Appleton before Cindy went home for Christmas. Nick then put a systems analyst named Tom Grainger, a youth of less than thirty and one of the best computer men I have met in all senses of the word "best" and "man," in charge of processing *The London Stage*. On November 22nd, Cindy had had Batch 1 for 37 days, Batch 3 for 11 days, and Batch 2 for 4 days. Philip's crew had finished Batch 6 and it was now expected in London.

Wednesday, 24 November: Send Muriel and Leonard suggestions for their presentation, announced for Tuesday, 28 December at 8:30 a.m. Assume Muriel has or will have her data momentarily. Write Cindy. Estimate that 6 and 9 will arrive in Appleton on about 8 December, the day her second term exams finish. Ask if she can stay over a few days and do Leff's data.

Thursday, 25 November: Thanksgiving.

Friday, 26 November: Cable Hong Kong asking for news of 6. Mail "Final Report on Phase 1 of the *London Stage* Project," 10 pp., to National Endowment for the Humanities

Saturday, 27 November: ———.

Sunday, 28 November: Visit friends in Surrey.

Monday, 29 November: Call Philip. He is sending Batch 6 and 9 tomorrow. Held 6 until 9 was done to save freight charge. Write Leonard that we may not be able to do his stuff unless Cindy can stay over after her exams.

Tuesday, 30 November: Write Cindy to cable if she can stay to process Leff's data.

Wednesday, 1 December: BOAC flight 833 carrying 6 and 9 arrived this morning. Sent to Manchester because of thick mist at Heathrow. Due at Heathrow 5:50 this afternoon. Terrific thunderstorm at 6. Called BOAC at 7— package there. 833 was last flight to land before the storm. They say five minutes later and it would have gone back to Manchester for the night. Ransom package for £5.50 ($13.75) plus freight charges. Unsympathetic customs officer.

Thursday, 2 December: 9 a.m. hand 6 and 9 to Tom Grainger. He is determined to beat the weekend by scanning steadily up to 3 p.m. Friday so as to meet 4 p.m. deadline at IBM Newman Street after which nothing can be done until Monday. Tom has found out how to catch initial full stop, by adjusting "line finder." So much for the voice on the intercom. Batch 9 scans perfectly. Decide to give air freight another chance. Cable Air Wisconsin how and when package is coming. Cable loyal friend and colleague, Elizabeth Forter, how and when package is coming. Warn everyone not to let North Central carry package to Green Bay. Cable telephone rendezvous for 7 p.m. next Wednesday with Cindy when her exams end.

Friday 3 December: Pick up ASCII tapes of 6 and 9 at Wembley and get them to Newman Street at 4 via British Rail, Bakerloo, Central, and Northern Underground Lines. Deposit input and output tapes in tape library. No one knows what customers agent is responsible for CSC. Call

Tom for name. Call name at North Row. On vacation. Has bequeathed job to another name. Explain problem: demonstration, seminar, Leff, Friedman, etc. He will call back in five minutes to give me job number. Does so. At 4:30 (approx.) go and get job using job number. Report shows too few blocks converted, abnormal program end. Call name at North Row. Line is busy. Call until 5— can't rouse any one. 5:10: Name calls me at Newman Street to find out how job went. I report my interpretation of job report. He decides it was the wrong program. Will make change and resubmit. Same rigamarole with job number. 5:45: Abnormal program end. North Row shut down for weekend. For want of a program at North Row on Friday a computer at Newman Street could not translate a tape from Wembley scanned from typing done in Hong Kong of a book printed in Vienna edited by scholars in DeKalb, Chicago, and Columbus to make it compatible with a computer in Appleton so that it could process their data for a seminar in Chicago, until Monday.

Saturday, 4 December: Cable from Cindy—she can do Leff's data if it comes before 12 December. Dean Stone writes that seminar attendance is expected to be high. Get printout from Cindy of ICISCAN output of Batch 2 on which she has marked a number of things causing her to believe something is wrong with CSC's tape. I think she may have used the wrong version of the program and that the tape is O.K.

Sunday, 5 December: Write Cindy asking her to try another approach. Tell her we cannot drop the ball now, etc. etc.

Monday, 6 December: It was for want of good tapes that all our ends were frustrated on Friday. The finicky IBM computer found physical flaws in CSC's tapes and so automatically aborted the ASCII-EBCDIC translation.

CSC reinscribes data on brand new tapes but too late to make four o'clock deadline at Newman Street today.

Tuesday, 7 December: North Row and Newman Street so slow I am unable to put tapes on any direct flights to Chicago at 1:30 p.m. Decide to wait for next direct flight at 1:30 Wednesday to be absolutely sure package is on plane and forestall Chicago handlers' excuse that package got stuck in New York.

Wednesday, 8 December: 1:30: Send Batches 6 and 9 under airwaybill 0653-8383 on BOAC Flight 569 arriving Chicago at 4:30 p.m. Air Wisconsin and Elizabeth Forter so informed by cable. 7 p.m. Wisconsin time: talked to Cindy on phone. Sent some kind of printouts to Mrs. Friedman this week. Cindy asked puzzling question: Are printouts for research or seminar? Confirm with Elizabeth that tapes arrived in Chicago at 4:30 under airwaybill 0653-8383 BOAC. Flight 569.

Thursday, 9 December: Receive letter from Muriel reporting phone call from Cindy to the effect that "she couldn't get the program to work." Cable phone rendezvous with Muriel Friday 6 p.m. her time to inquire further.

Friday, 10 December: Elizabeth cables "Tapes grounded Green Bay customs Rescue Monday." Call Muriel. Answers phone but never got cable. Says printout has lots of irrelevant plays on it. Can't figure out why. Either can I.

Saturday, 11 December: 11 p.m.: Talk to Cindy. SELECT option of ITEMGET won't work. Made printouts for Mrs. Friedman by SORTMERGing everything in Batch 1 and tearing out unwanted data by hand, i.e. manual SELECT option. Hasn't got to Batches 2 and 3 yet. In response to my distress she says, "You hired me for an operator, not a programmer. Mr. Church says as far as he knows Will never ran a batch through the whole system before he left."

I put the phone back on the hook about 11:15 that night. In due course Kay and I went to bed, but I didn't sleep until about four. I now for the first time saw what Will and Cindy had been trying to accomplish in Appleton instead of processing data for Muriel Friedman and Leonard Leff. Bits and pieces of information now began to register and form a coherent pattern. In fact none of the dozens of messages I had sent since leaving Appleton had achieved the desired effect because I had never once directly and clearly contradicted one particular basic assumption of theirs that I could not even conceive of, simply because it stood square in the way of what I desired most. Since this assumption was never challenged, it persisted, fostering a course of action contrary to everything I sought to accomplish.

I now realized that I had been demanding that two very conscientious people do something totally counter to all their training. I had wanted them, although this wasn't at all the way I looked at it, to do a poor piece of work, to make shoddy merchandise, to perpetrate error. We knew that our typed and scanned text would contain many mistakes, and that some of these would cause many ladder failures. If a typist makes a mistake in a particular date dozens of ladder references over a long span of time will fail. Will and Cindy were well aware of the damage a few errors could do and since ICISCAN did a good job of reporting errors, they knew there were a good number. It was impossible for them to believe, I deduced in the night, that bona fide scholars could have any commerce with error, especially in presentations to the scholarly community as a whole. What they needed to know was that I *recognized* precisely how unprofessional it is to propagate error and how heinous a crime I wanted them to commit. Because they did not know this, my talk of getting printouts to Muriel and Leonard as fast as possible must have been brushed aside as irrelevant. They must reason that if I knew what they knew about the data I would not be thinking about printouts.

Even now, I fear I may not be able to make my readers understand why, in this case, the release of erroneous documents would not be a scholarly crime. In the first place, neither Muriel nor Leonard had been offered altogether correct information; I knew I couldn't promise this. In the second place, as specialists in that very material, they were the ones most qualified to detect errors and avoid jumping to false conclusions. In the third place, Muriel was not giving a paper on O'Keefe's plays and Leonard was not giving a paper on the meaning of Sheridan's casting; they were explaining how computer arrangements of cast lists could expedite a scholar's research. Cindy's puzzling question about whether the printouts were for research or the seminar now made perfect sense. They were for the seminar, of course. Only then did she sense that we had been working at cross purposes. Finally, what I wanted to demonstrate above all was that our programs worked. If our programs worked (and tonight it seemed almost certain they didn't) nothing could prove it better than printouts like Leff's and Mrs. Friedman's.

I had thought that we all knew this. The difference in basic premises explained an offcourse correspondence between Will and Leonard that had come to light just as Will was about to leave. After completing his editing, Leonard sent Will on my suggestion the list of plays he wished to have casts of. Will wrote back saying that most of the data was not available yet. At that, Leonard wrote that he was in no hurry. At that time, Leonard didn't know that he was in a hurry, because he didn't know that there might be a seminar and that he probably would be in it. He wasn't invited until September. But Will, who until now had been taking Leonard's needs into account, now pushed them off the bottom of the priority scale. I had no knowledge of this correspondence until late September, when Will remarked casually in a letter that Leff was in no hurry for his data. The remark put me in a state of consternation that prompted me to ask Will, in our telephone conference of the 30th of September, how he knew. Will immediately sent me the whole correspondence. I then wrote Leonard about the seminar, about the same time as David Mann did, and promised him the careers of Sheridan's actors before long. Cindy, who took over on the 15th of October, apparently absorbed little of the background for the seminar, amid other concerns of the transfer. What came home to her in her sessions with Will was the importance of weeding out errors; hence she could write on the 10th of November: "I've had no problems with the programs thus far, but I thought I'd tell you that the process is more time-consuming than I thought it would be (especially ICIFIX)—so, even if more tapes did come in, I doubt that I'd be able to process them by the end of term one. Thus, I'd appreciate it if you could let me know what must be done by Christmas (e.g., the MLA convention stuff)."

Having labored with ICIFIX, myself, I knew what she meant. It could take as long as 20 minutes to find out and fix one tiny error in the computerized text. I immediately wrote that printouts were absolute top priority and that it was much too late for all that ICIFIXing now. Full speed ahead and damn the mistakes. It was now November 10th, however, with final exams only three weeks off. The *London Stage* Information Bank had consumed too much study time already, it was now too late for Cindy to do much of anything. Hence she did not find out until the first week in December that she couldn't, because she hadn't tried to, get the final steps of the system to work at all.

At about ten Sunday morning after a few hours of fitful sleep, dreaming of EBCDIC and ICIFIX, I was wide awake again, feeling a strong compulsion to do something. A possible reason why the SELECT option of ITEMGET wouldn't work had come to me in the night. At about 11 Kay woke up. I said, "I can't think of anything to do but fly to Appleton." She said, "Why don't you fly to Appleton, then. You've tried everything else." "Cindy says I didn't hire her for a programmer and she's right. Heaven knows where Will is. I'm not a programmer either but I am the only one who possibly can salvage something, and I must try to." I then viewed the proposition in the moral light, which was the best light you could view it in because it certainly wasn't practical. "We owe it to the people who have backed us with all this money and all this work. If the project falls on its face at this point, especially after all the optimistic reports I've been circulating, I will be rightly condemned for taking money under false pretenses." I was over-dramatizing, but there was some truth in this. "Also, I can't stand the thought that after all we've been through we don't have anything. Not one single thing. Close but no cigar. If I go back I can find Will and get him working on it. Cindy can't do all that." And finally we summed it up this way: "How will we feel ten years from now thinking that we might have been able to pull it off. But we didn't for want of an airplane trip." This would be the only transoceanic flight that anyone in our whole family connection had ever taken without planning for it at least a year, but who can measure the value of an easy conscience? We both knew it was cheap at the price of a flight to Appleton.

Without hurrying unduly I made the 1:30 plane to Chicago and was with Cindy in the subterranean vaults of the Institute at 8 that evening (2 a.m. London time). She was happy. "After I hung up last night," she said, "I thought of a reason why the SELECT option of ITEM-GET doesn't work." "The capitalization?" I asked. "Right. So I called Will in Chapel Hill and asked him whether the parameter cards with Mrs. Friedman's titles had to have slashes in front of the capital letters or not in order to work. He said it was one way or the other. Our cards don't have slashes so I punched up a new deck last night with slashes and tried them on some of Batch 1. It worked. At least I think it worked, if it's O.K. that some titles didn't drop." I thought it was O.K.

And so it was that on the evening of December 12th, while the disk thunked and the tapes whirred, the printer ripped off sheet after sheet of O'Keefe's casts in alphabetical order by play and in chronological order by cast for a full three-quarters of an hour. Nothing but O'Keefe casts. And so many I could not believe that the ladder could have retrieved so many, alphabetized by play and listed in chronological order. The computer ripped out page after page after page as if it would never stop. I was overcome and the print looked blurred as I watched it go by.

Monday afternoon, having returned to the absurd workaday world I met the circuit-riding customs agent and cleared the tapes I'd sent the previous Tuesday. That evening Cindy and I made the printouts to Leonard's specifications and next morning I flew back to England. Between planes at O'Hare I presented Muriel Friedman with her printouts and with Leonard Leff's in care of her.

On my return to London a Christmas card awaited me. In a gold frame was mounted an ivory sheet of watered silk on which a red and gold dragon held a Chinese lantern in its mouth bearing four Chinese characters. Underneath was inscribed the legend "Season's Greetings." Inside was a handwritten message: "Dear Professor Ben and Family, With best Wishes For a Merry Christmas and A Happy New Year. Love, Philip." I received that message and have taken it to heart.

CHAPTER VIII

AN OVERVIEW

The Author reflects on his Experiences: among other things touching upon a Cybernetic View of the London Stage Information Bank; *Incompatibilities, Catches of Computing, and Interfaces; an English Professor's Information Theory; a Dialectical Approach to Programming; and peaceful Uses of Computers.*

It is now over a year since Cindy and I watched the printouts cascading forth and since Philip sent his love. Phase two is under way and final editing proceeds. Although the end-product was pretty much what I started out to get in May of 1970, I continually marvel at the route I took to reach that end. And although it has been possible to tell what happened episode by episode I am still unable to comprehend as a whole the process by which I reached it. So many people and institutions were involved, so many were the ways in which they interacted, so many chances for failure lay in wait, not the least of which was my own ignorance of data processing and my inexperience with it. What a miracle that I made no fatal error! What luck that so many accidents fell in with the master plan—like John Chan's spur of the moment phone call about terminals that serendipitously introduced me to China Data Corporation, or the sudden materialization of Mrs. Friedman at the point when I needed an editor and she needed to comb *The London Stage* for performances of O'Keefe's plays! How great a number and diversity of people and groups had to cooperate with me in pursuance of their own private and even alien goals. How could all these criss-crossing paths lead to one place?

In the course of my peregrinations in computerland I often heard the name of Norbert Wiener and, attached to it, the word "cybernetics." Understanding that cybernetics had something to do with the way organizations work, I read Wiener's book *The Human Use of Human Beings,* in hopes that it might help to explain the inchoate world of pullings and haulings that comprised the *London Stage* project. Indeed I think it does. Essentially what Wiener does is to relate entropy, which I comprehend only dimly when I comprehend it at all; feedback, which is what a thermostat does; information, which I have taken too much for granted; and probability, which has always been with us.

Entropy, we are told, is what you get when the second law of thermodynamics has done its relentless work. It means, a physicist friend of mine tells me, that you can't win, you can't break even, and you can't get out of the game. The game is man versus chaos. For strength to go on, all life depends on transfer of energy from one body of matter to another. From the sun to the earth, from minerals to vegetables, from vegetables to animals, in countless ways energy powers the system of the world by passing from things that have more of it to things that have less. But when the sun cools to the temperature of the earth, a desolate state of equilibrium will occur, in which there is no difference in energy level to enable transfer. In this state of affairs all motion is random, directionless, useless, purpose-less, and absolutely controlled by the laws of chance or probability, like the motion of gas molecules in an iron box kept at a constant temperature or a coin endlessly tossed until the deviation in the proportion of heads to tails be-comes infinitesimal and vanishes.

Against this ever-increasing entropy purposeful islands of organization hold out by controlling those waterfalls of energy transfer that still exist. While differences in energy levels persist, such islands are not only possible, but can even for a time reverse the inexorable levelling process. You and I are such islands, and so is an anthill, and, in some degree, the United States; or, I dare to think, the *London Stage* project. These islands, moreover, cannot organize without a blueprint. For you and me, and for the ants, it is our genes; for the United States it is the Consti-tution. And for the *London Stage* project? Would it be the Specs? The grand general term for such guides to purpose-ful operation is information.

In *The Human Use of Human Beings*, Wiener calmly makes what is to me a hair-raising observation, all the more hair-raising because it is obvious once you see it, that "We are not stuff that abides, but patterns that per-petuate themselves. A pattern is a message." Me today is the aggregation of an entirely different set of molecules from me yesterday. "We are but whirlpools in a river of ever-flowing water." I am a message sent to the entropic flux. And as if this were not enough, because I can transmit my will by letter, telephone, or television, the message that is me cannot even be said to occupy my own body. If an architect in Paris can cause a building of his design to materialize in New York, can he be said to "live" in New York? Thus Wiener establishes that information is the soul of any organ, organism, or organization identifiable as such, and the soul is not the body and the soul is not confined to the body.

Besides being a message, I am a sender and receiver of messages. Hereon hangs another observation of Wiener's, hitherto not obvious to me—the part played by feedback in the organic unit's capacity to control itself. I am fitted out with five senses with which to receive signals from the world. Sight feeds back to me the degree to which my car's course is faithful to its proper lane. Smell tells me whether the toast is burning. Machines use feedback, too. The furnace reads a thermostat to find out how well it is doing, and computer programs continually test the present state of a process to decide what to do next.

Wiener presents us with a universe tending toward chaos and eternal night, in which information in control of energy fights to establish order and light. Verily, "In the beginning was the word." It follows inexorably that whatever impedes a message, be that message feedback or feedforward, spreads disorder. At this point Wiener's reasoning takes what for an English teacher is a brilliant step. If messages impose order on a probabilistic world, then, he says, the more improbable a message is the more information it contains. If someone shouts fire in a building I inhabit, since it is a word I almost never hear shouted in that context, it does indeed qualify as improbable and certainly the information has great value to me. It follows that the most likely and probable words and phrases that I hear have the least value as information. And I who have for twenty-five years remonstrated with red pencil and pleading voice, humbly, endlessly, fruitlessly, and often ridiculously, against clichés, jargon, and fuzziness may now hear myself called Doctor without a twinge of guilt and don the white coat of scientifically proven fact. The "signal-to-noise ratio" that I used to see in ratings of radio sets is, when applied to language, the information-to-gobbledygook ratio.

Finally, all this reasoning—from entropy to probability to messages to feedback to noise—leads to cybernetics, the word which Wiener coined from the Greek word for steersman, the science of steering things, the science of control, the study of how anything imaginable is kept on the right track. In hopes of understanding the *London Stage* project, I found myself one day attempting to chart cybernetically the various lines of control that evolved in the process of producing Muriel's and Leonard's printouts. Some postWienerians would call my activity "systems analysis," I suppose, but I believe one is supposed to do the analyzing *before* doing the work, not after. As I conduct systems analysis, it does at least help to identify one's mistakes. For the reader's amusement—close scrutiny will not repay the time it takes—I include as Figure 10 the diagram of the *London Stage* System that I was after many false starts at last able to draw. Certainly this chart does not begin to show forth the entangled multitude of strands that went into the final fabric. But it may provide a visual suggestion of the true complexity.

Observe that the seven major transformations of the text of *The London Stage* on its way to Leonard and Muriel fall down the right side of the page and are marked "Flow of data." I say "fall" in faithfulness to the cybernetic idea, which tells me that the energy consumed in making those printouts has reduced the heat of the sun. On my chart I have shown the forces that control the transfer of energy to those printouts operating from left to right and labelled "Flow of control," because the steersmen on the right are responsible to the steersmen on the left.

Obviously the Specs, by which we hoped to build the best service we could imagine for our potential users out of the text, machines, money, manpower, and time at our disposal, are the central controlling document. All our major decisions and deliberations are reflected in the Specs,

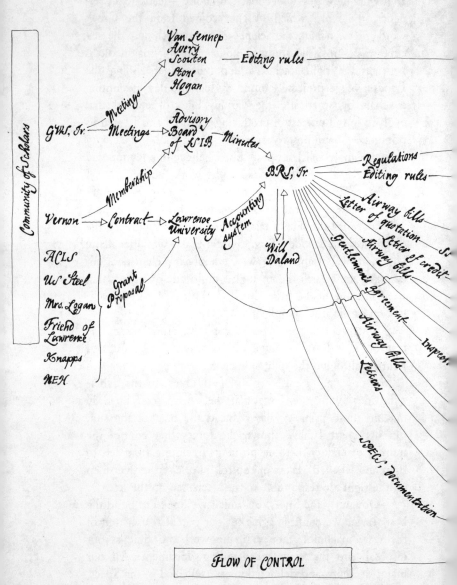

FIGURE 10

Medium of transport or transform			FLOW OF DATA
			Playbills, newspapers, letters, diaries
	Publishing		The London Stage, 1660–1800
The mails		Planes	Pages for editing
Muriel, Leonard Marcus, Mark Schneider children		Pencils	Pages for typing
The mails Air Wisconsin, Flying Tigers		Planes	Pages in Hong Kong
China data	Hong Kong DP		Pages in OCRB
First National, Appleton	First Wisconsin, Milwaukee	Hong Kong National Bank	Deposit
BOAC			
Broker	H.M. Customs	Clearance	OCRB in London
CSC		Scanner	BCD tape
IBM		Program	EBCDIC tape
BOAC			
Broker	U.S. Customs		EBCDIC in Appleton
Cindy	GENER1, ICIFIX, ICISCAN, STRUCTUR, LADDER, ITEMGET, SORT, FORMAT		Printouts

and the more we labored over them the more they came to describe the possible. Will knew from the start that computer projects require far-reaching, explicit, and imaginative advanced planning. By "imaginative" I do not mean anything so fashionable as "poetic," "artistic," or "creative." I mean simply having the capacity to prophesy what things are likely to happen. Much waste might have been avoided if I had realized this sooner.

But the Specs were only one of many written documents by which our course was steered. There were customs regulations, airwaybills, minutes of meetings, grant proposals, editing rules, and the letter of credit, to name a few of the others. In addition—and on my chart I had not space or ingenuity to show all of them—there were a great many lines of feedback reversely moving in various ways to correct steering errors. Some functioned well, some poorly and some were only available if needed. If, for example, the academic community in some way changed the course of events by its responses to my newsletter, I was not aware of its influence, unless one may say that the low amplitude and low signal-to-noise ratio of the responses confirmed my opinion that actor biographies and role histories were their principal need. I regret that Philip Hui did not feed back to me right away some news of the great hardship imposed by our specification that every page should be full to the 75th character of the 30th line. Having editors supply me with feedback in the form of tests seems to have established good communication between us. Corporation S's test sample divulged in time their scanners' inability to register two spaces, and I personally fed back to CSC in London more than one batch when their scanners' rate of accuracy slumped. But Cindy Percak's hesitation about writing letters caused her processing to veer off course. Both the presence of feedback in the system and its absence show how vitally important it is.

Looking at my chart I can quickly understand why lots of computer rooms I've seen have signs in them, sometimes carved in marble, that say "Nothing is as easy as it looks." When I rose up at meetings to ask for the computerizing of *The London Stage, 1660–1800,* I thought only of the fact that identifying names and sorting things was a trivial exercise for a computer. I had no idea that *The London Stage* was as various and intractable a document as Will and I found it to be when we tried to write the Specs. Nor did I realize how difficult programming such a motley conglomeration of facts would be. It was almost daily feedbetween of Will and me that kept programming and text-processing on the track. In those innocent days before I fell into data processing, I knew I would have to know more about computers than I did, but I had no inkling that I would have to know as much about such things as contracts, fund-raising, customs clearance, air freight, accountancy, international banking, printing, and the inscrutable East as I eventually had to. Nor could I ever have imagined that most of my time would be taken up with such things as finding out how to get an optical scanner to distinguish capital *O* from zero, writing clear typing instructions that were also exhaustive, developing an editing system for which there was room on the page, persuading data-processing firms to meet declared standards, and explaining to sales representatives what their products were.

This kind of optimistic faith that what is conceivable on a computer can easily be accomplished is by no means peculiar to me. Most people who have close relationships to computing habitually lunge blindly ahead from one disaster to another, bloody and happy, sure that success is only one day or week away—certainly not more than a month. One reason for this optimism must be that, barring occasional strays like me, most computing people are young—in their twenties or thirties. I rarely meet anyone as old as I am in a computer room. When I objected recently that a piece of equipment ordered in January and promised in April was repromised in May and when May ran out repromised in the middle of June and when the middle of June passed repromised next week and I never expected to get it, a friend who had seen a lot more computing than I told me to take courage, because the units of time were getting smaller with each promise. Pretty soon it would just have to arrive. And so it did, in the middle of that next week. An older and wiser company would have promised July and delivered on time, but hope springs eternal in the computing breast.

Being dreamers by historical definition—dropouts from Europe looking for the Fountain of Youth, the New Jerusalem, streets paved with gold, and Freedom—we Americans are perhaps readier than people of older countries to leap at the chance offered by computers to escape the limitations of the flesh, more impatient with delay, and less disheartened by failure. Our history even testifies that we have had some success in changing aspects of nature and society that stood in the way to a better world. I wonder if this historical factor also contributes to the computer industry's habit of promising more than it can deliver.

Even though I have been seasoned in many of life's campaigns, and have long ceased to expect my tomatoes to ripen before the Wisconsin frost or my students to believe me when I tell them that there is no such thing as "a media," and though I consider myself wise in the ways of the world, I am still a fool about computing. Country people used to call the Montgomery Ward catalogue "the wish book." We should call the computer "the wish machine." I understand that before the computer was much more than a gleam in electronic engineers' eyes, the great mathematical thinker Turing had proved mathematically that the programmable digital machine then under develop' ment was indeed a universal machine, and could do any' thing if supplied the necessary information and given the proper tools. He proved that it could not be proved that a programmable machine could not think. Soon automatic translation, automatic indexing, and automatic teaching projects were in full swing. Billions of taxpayers' dollars were poured into them. After twenty-five years of failure, enthusiasm for such work has considerably diminished, public funds are drying up, and some of the workers have quietly shifted their sights to lesser targets. But I imagine that most of them would rather be burned at the stake than give up the principle that computers can do anything.

By searching my own soul, I think I can understand some of the reasons for this optimism. Anyone who knows the least bit about computing can immediately and plainly see, exactly as Turing saw, how an imaginary computer can achieve an imaginary task, even to the extent of describing the imaginary algorithm that will do it without fail. (An algorithm, the lay reader may wish to know, is, according to IBM Manual GC20-1699-1, "a prescribed set of well defined rules for the solution of a problem in a finite number of steps." The word is not derived from "algos," the Greek word for pain, as one might surmise, but from "al-Khuwarizmi," an Arabic mathematician of the 9th century A.D. who apparently specialized in al-Khu' warizms.)

Looking back at all the unexpected snags that I en' countered, I note how much grief was caused by my taking estimates of feasibility at face value. Machines did not meet specifications, schedules could not be met. And it wasn't for lack of trying. I myself promised Muriel her printouts three months before I was able to deliver them. I did so partly from ignorance, but partly because I, too, confused the machine of my dreams with the machine in the computer room. So blinded, I could not possibly have foreseen that before I delivered Muriel's printouts I would have to modify eight typing elements, that the mails would fail in the swift completion of their appointed rounds, that the Specs would misguide Philip, and that the scanner would have so much trouble reading a full stop at the beginning of a line.

Now, as the algesic experiences of several years have taught me, there's a long, long trail a-winding between imaginary algorithms and viable computer processes. First of all, real machines can't perform a tenth as well as imaginary machines; not even a thousandth as well as some people's imaginary machines, and it is not machines but the people who feed and direct them and make up for their deficiencies—Will Daland, Muriel Friedman, Cindy Luk, Gerry Dowdy, Tom Grainger, and Cindy Percak—who really guide us to the land of our dreams where the nightingale is singing and the fair moon beams, if indeed it is possible to get there. The computer only seems like an escape from the limits of mortality. Indeed its impassive, mechanical perfection provides an excellent dramatic backdrop for the ridiculous slapstick pratfalls of its human manipulators. It plays Gulliver to our Lilliputian antics.

Besides the fact that computer people tend to be dreamers, three other special features of the industry serve to multiply exponentially the likelihood of overreaching: the sheer number of people involved, the newness of computing, and the effect of computing on the psyche of those who compute.

Computer people are so machine-oriented that they fail to take account of the large part played by human beings in the accomplishment of even the smallest computing task. As my chart shows, hundreds of people, perhaps thousands, if we include the people required to accomplish a transatlantic flight, had to cooperate in order to produce Muriel's and Leonard's printouts. Human cooperation would be a large factor even if only one computer center were involved. Programmers depend on systems men, hardware needs maintenance men, data preparation involves a manager and workers. On the other hand, scholarly work as I knew it usually involved simply the scholar and a few steadfast librarians. A new corollary of Murphy's Law suggests itself: "The number of things that can go wrong is directly proportional to the number of people involved in the process."

The problem that computing poses for all the people connected with it is compounded exponentially by the fact that the computer is a new machine and, moreover, a universal new machine. Neither British nor American customs had a category for scanner input, so the former called it typescript and the latter called it data-processing forms, and I waited endlessly while agents consulted each other and thumbed through manuals. Another exponential factor is added to the complexity of computer problems by the fact that it is a universal machine: given the tools, the resources, and the program, it can do anything. And anything is what computers are doing. Consequently my attempt to clarify matters for customs agents by explaining that I needed this typing from Hong Kong for a research project in English literature, but that it wasn't a manuscript for a book or transcripts of foreign documents, only served to mystify them further. Customs regulations not only have to adjust to a new line of products from a new industry; they also have to adjust to a new line of products from every form of human enterprise—because computers can do anybody's work (some of anybody's work). In the jargon of the trade, adjusting to new hardware is easy compared to the difficulty of adjusting to the hundreds and thousands of new applications.

As Figure 10 shows, the outcome of the project depended a lot more on the coordination of human effort than it did on writing programs for a particular machine. Truly, getting ready to run the program is the part of the iceberg that is under water. Even getting ready to write the program, as Will's and my long tussle over the Specs proves, is a major preliminary task. A contradiction appears to be looming here, to the effect that the best labor-saving machine ever invented requires far more human help than its far less capable predecessors. If, in the end, the *London Stage* Information Bank can do the work of twenty scholars working twenty years in only twenty minutes, it may well require several times that much work to get it in motion. For this sobering thought there are two consolations. The twenty scholars would never have undertaken the work done by the computer in twenty minutes because it would have been unthinkably dull and endless, and the benefit uncertain; and the labor of getting ready to use the machine ensures that, contrary to popular opinion, the computer will not cause unemployment. Because *The London Stage* is accessible, siftable, and sortable by computer, research is feasible that was never before attempted: we can study trends (the rise of pantomime; the interest in Shakespeare; the rise and fall of theatres; the decline of the drama); we can look for patterns (In what ways is one season like another? What is a typical stage career like? To what extent do actors specialize? What is the effect of the repertory system?). There's too much information about 18th century theatre; without computer help we can't see the forest for the trees.

Returning to the incorrigible tendency of computer people to overreach the bounds of the possible, I believe that perhaps the psychological effect of the computer on the computor (the one who computes) may be partly to blame for it. Although man is by nature a social animal, as Aristotle declared, this trait may not be as true of computer people, if by "social" we mean "happiest in the company of his fellow creatures." Anyone who has spent much time with computers knows how entertaining, witty, unpredictable, and intellectually challenging they can be, how gratifying is their instant obedience, how scrutable their simple psychology, how comfortably even their most surprising aberrations ultimately conform to explicit rules. In short, it is not surprising that some people really prefer the company of computers to that of human beings. I have read the following statement in a book about computers and society:

With computers providing vast, as yet unimagined synthetic worlds of pleasures to explore, why engage in the already marginal exploration of this all too unsatisfactory world . . . ? Recall how far many of us have already gone into music, games, and programming for the love of programming with only the slightest regard for utility. Recall the attractiveness of a world in which all the basic rules are known, where the goals may be set arbitrarily and cleanly. . . . Don't sell the human too short in his willingness to enjoy life. With the ability to make synthetic worlds to fit his desires, far beyond what amateur daydreaming can do, worlds where there is a real intellectual challenge and a sense of accomplishment that transcends any reward that mere daydreaming can offer, think how far many people will choose to go.*

This quotation does not come from a book of science fiction but from an introductory textbook of computing. It is perfectly innocent of irony. After Gulliver's sojourn with

* Richard W. Hamming, *Computers and Society* (New York: McGraw-Hill, 1972), p. 191. Copyright © 1972 by McGraw-Hill Book Co.; reprinted by permission.

the absolutely rational Houyhnhnms, he could not stand his wife and children anymore, but spent most of his time in the barn with his horses.

Cases of almost psychopathic withdrawal can be observed wherever there are computers. But it is not restricted to computer bums. The rise of specialization in business and the professions has a similar isolating effect. The specialist inevitably carves out a monopoly on the thing he does; he becomes irreplaceable. Now not only his special knowledge maroons him on a solitary isle, but also his power. He has become so necessary to some organization's welfare that he needs no friends. He can indulge whatever antisocial tendencies he has without endangering his security. "I am a rock," he can sing, with Simon and Garfunkel. His favorite companions, if his work does not fill his life, are the happy few who know enough to talk about his work. His home is his profession—not his house, his town, or his business (as Tofler has so well observed in *Future Shock*). Some specialists' specialties are like electric trains. But the train, instead of being their avocation, is their vocation. Work is play. When I spend a weekend at the office with the seven or eight others who habitually devote their spare time to research, I have often wondered, thinking of the fatherless children and husbandless wives, if we are not all just playing with our electric trains. We may think of ourselves as Alexander Fleming discovering penicillin, but what is our real motive? Life inside the office often is less taxing than life outside. It doesn't involve people, it doesn't talk back, and it's easy to do. But the computer is the best electric train ever made.

Because the computer is a universal machine, it creates specialists faster than any previous discovery. In fact the programmer who designs a system of the size required for *The London Stage* may well become the only person who knows how it works, can fix it if it develops a bug, or can alter it for new conditions. Given the job of modifying another programmer's work, a programmer will often find it faster to rewrite the whole program. The *London Stage* programs are about as long as *Paradise Lost*, and nearly as hard to write. Some programs may be as long as *War and Peace* and just as comprehensive. Owners cry out desperately for Documentation, but is easy to see why programmers hate to document: it's dull work and—if they do their job as thoroughly as they should— it makes them dispensable.

Social isolation and irresponsibility are further encouraged by the tone of the times. Never in American history has the individual rated so high and society so low. We must do our own thing, dress our own way, walk to a different drummer from everyone else. Those who display contempt for groups and institutions are greeted with the utmost respect. Thoreau is the model. I doubt, however, that the real Thoreau would ever have found his Walden in a computer room, where so many modern hermits have holed up.

What I seem to have arrived at is that although the newness of computing, the great diversity of computer applications, specialization, and the tone of the times all contribute to greater individualism, production of computer output seems to require more social activity, organization, and cooperation than any form of production hitherto engaged in. It requires more willing cooperation, more selfless devotion to the task assigned, not less, than previous kinds of production. There is not much I can do about antisocial forces in the computing trade except to decry them. But as an English teacher looking at computing from outside, I cannot help making a few suggestions about how communication between those who compute may be improved.

Returning once more to my flowchart of the *London Stage* System, the reader will note that the labels on the "Flow of control" arrows designate the media (Latin for "mediums") of control used by the various agents of control. Almost all of these media, he will see at a glance, are written documents of some sort: contracts, proposals, letters of quotation, specifications, rules. There were many phone calls and letters but the most important and powerful media of control were written down.

I am not aware that the term "interface" has currency in information theory. If it doesn't, I think it should have. My three dictionaries of computer terms—IBM, *Datamation*, and Penguin—all agree that an interface is what occurs at the boundary between two systems, usually the computer and its input and output peripherals. The two systems are essentially incompatible: a printer operating a lot of little hammers, a computer putting out electrical impulses. Or a tape drive reading magnetic spots to a computer desiring electronic impulses. The interface, like Janus, looks both ways, translating from one mode to the other. It is a law of information science, I have learned, that some information is always lost in transmission. Is it perhaps not true that more of it is lost at the interface than anywhere else? Certainly this is true of communication between human systems. Translation from one language to another, we know, always involves a greater loss than transmission of the message in its own language. If the analogy of translation holds true for electronic interfaces, may we not then single out interfaces as the most error-prone parts of a communication line?

They certainly are if we use "interface" metaphorically, as is so often done these days. If, for instance, the separate

systems are the persons and groups of my *London Stage*
flowchart and the interfaces are the documents acting as
media of control, then undeniably the loci of greatest
potential loss are the media which translate one system to the
other. The Specs, to take the foremost example, had to
translate information from a programming environment to
a typing environment. We have seen what happens when
such translation fails, when transfer from one mode of
operation, one set of assumptions, to another, not just from
English to Chinese, is imperfect. Generalizing from the
London Stage project to the production of computer output everywhere, we observe that documents in what computer men call natural language (to distinguish it from
programming or artificial language) do most of the work in
holding incompatible elements of social (as distinct from
individual) systems together.

It is ironic, even tragic, that a community which trea-
sures and refines artificial languages (FORTRAN, PL/1,
BASIC, and so forth) should set so little store by natural
language that English becomes a more impoverished and
weaker vehicle of communication among those who compute, while artificial languages become richer and more
powerful. We can talk to our machines better than we can
talk to ourselves.

Consider for a moment Wiener's doctrine that the least
probable message contains the most information; and con-
versely, that the most probable message contains the least
information. This tells us that jargon is to be avoided at all
costs. What is jargon? To speak jargon is to make sounds
for the purpose of announcing that one belongs to a certain
class of person: educator, physicist, baseball player, ecolo-
gist, civil servant, hairdresser, clubwoman, though the last
one or two probably fall more into the habit of clichés, the
jargon of small talk. Utterances in jargon are like bird calls:

they identify the species and little more. Consider this passage from an article entitled "The User Interface for Interactive Bibliographic Searching":

During the last ten years Interactive Bibliographical Search and Retrieval (IBSR) systems have progressed from the drawing boards, through prototype models, to operational status. [Once we didn't have interactive bibliographic searching systems, now we do.] Yet knowledge about the blend of ingredients that produces a comfortable man-machine interface is still at the anecdotal level. [Everybody's talking about the makeup of easy-to-use systems, but nobody knows much.] The reasons for the lack of reliable evidence are numerous. [Uh-huh.] Experimental subjects, whose behavior can be controlled, tend to react differently than spontaneous searchers. Spontaneous searching behavior cannot be translated into usable design data unless efficient monitors and sophisticated data analyzers are built into operational IBSR systems. Not only are monitors and analyzers expensive and little understood; their use cannot be justified if the man-machine interface cannot be improved. Few systems existing today can be modified easily. [Controlled experimental subjects don't behave like real ones. You can't study real ones without putting monitors and analyzers in the programs. Nobody knows how to make a good monitor or analyzer. Monitors and analyzers are expensive. Their use cannot be justified unless the IBSR system can be improved.] Can we deduce user preferences, if not for features then at least for systems? Unfortunately few institutions have been able to provide their searchers with access to more than one system. Consequently, interface design recommendations cannot be formulated today without tapping intuitively-based opinions. [Several ideas have been left out here, but apparently this means: "If real searchers could try many systems, and tell us which they liked best, we could deduce which features of the systems were most useful. But nobody is able to try this method (for some unstated reason). Consequently, we will ask some people what they think."]

Clearly it was not the purpose of this paragraph to communicate anything improbable and new about IBSR, but simply to make a noise like an information scientist, to caress the ears of other information scientists and lull them into uncritical acceptance. If outsiders are unable to enjoy the noises, that only adds to the cosy feeling. How glamorous the words are! What thrilling arcana they refer to! "Drawing board," "prototype," "man-machine interface," "operational status," "usable design data," "intuitively-based." What a privilege to be able to use and recognize this splendid terminology!

A far more noisy feature of pseudoscientific lingo is its typical sentence structure. The problem is not that too many technologists use bad grammar, but that they try to avoid it altogether. The result is a certain "izziness" of style. For example:

It has been argued that the present-day retrieval thesaurus construction and maintenance rules and conventions are not theoretically based.

In this statement (which comes, unfortunately, from a journal of information science), strings of nouns and parts of the verb "to be" take the place of true adjectives, prepositions, and action verbs. With missing muscles and sinews in place, the sentence would read something like this:

I have argued that modern rules for the construction and maintenance of thesauri which are used for retrieval of information have no theoretical basis.

Now the passive voice does not appear in the main clause. The passive, of course, being nothing but "to be" and a verb demoted to adjective status as a past participle, creates most of the izziness of scientific prose.

Scientists assume that they write this way to keep from being subjective. But the pose of objectivity develops the habit of preferring the passive whether it's needed for avoiding "I" or not. I propose that this is fooling nobody, that it causes weakness, vagueness, irresponsibility, and ambiguity. For example, in the original sentence, if you didn't know that the author had been arguing for retrieval thesauri based on theory, you might think that others were arguing it. So far, we have only a lamentable ambiguity. However, the ambiguity is not always innocent. Because it has no subject, the passive voice allows an author to duck responsibility: he doesn't have to say who or what did the thing. He can write, for example, that the "rules" referred to "are not based" and avoid accusing any specific persons of acting without a basis. Naming the guilty group makes possible an even stronger sentence than my first version:

I have argued that information scientists do not at present base their rules for constructing and maintaining retrieval thesauri on any theory.

Now, two of the original nouns, "construction" and "maintenance," are gone and two verbal nouns, "constructing" and "maintaining," take their place, so that the guilty "information scientists" are also doing something, which adds a tiny bit to the information content. The cowardly original sentence had only the potential of supplying this much information.

Another tendency is using nouns even for verbs—the ultimate izzyness. The goal of some technologists is apparently to write sentences composed entirely of concepts, as empty as possible of messy human activity. If the verb can be a concept, too, the rape of natural language is more complete and satisfying. I recently heard an after-dinner speaker who was introduced as a professional futurist. Wearing a yellow tie and purple pants, he exuded jovial sociability, but his speech began something like this: "I wanna image for you the following real-time scenario." If he is a futurist, I hope he is not a sign of what the future holds in store.

The point I want to make is that English is, as computer people say of this or that programming language, "a powerful language" too. It is exceedingly "generalized" in scope, it has a copious "instruction set," lots of useful "subroutines," a flexible syntax, and rules for "assembly" that a child can learn. Unfortunately, it must be "compiled" "by hand." But for transmission of information from one human being to another, it cannot be excelled.

To prevent extreme loss of information at the boundary between two social environments requires not only full use of the powers of English, but something more difficult to attain. The *London Stage* project required interfacing between a number of pairs of essentially different social environments: Technology/scholarship, science/art, research/business, United States/Hong Kong/England, computer science/*The London Stage*. The something more, included always in the advice of English teachers and in the admonitions of writing handbooks, is for the sender of messages to take into account the receiver's circumstances, basic assumptions, ignorance, and knowledge. The main reason for poor transmission across environmental boundaries is failure to translate beforehand into the terms of existence holding sway at the other end. To bridge the gap what we need is contained in a word that has been so badly obfuscated by misuse that I hate to use it now: imagination. To develop the imagination, I know of no better exercise than the reading of imaginative literature. Shelley has anticipated what I want to say in his *Defence of Poetry*, where he talks of poetry's moral effect. "A man," he says, "to be greatly good, must imagine intensely and comprehensively; he must put himself in the place of another and of many others. . . . Poetry enlarges the circumference of the imagination by replenishing it with thoughts of ever new delight. . . . Poetry strengthens the faculty which is the organ of the moral nature of man in the same manner as exercise strengthens a limb." This same organ, I maintain, is the best one for creating interfaces: machine-machine, man-machine, or man-man.

In a computer project the man-machine interface is a most important one. In the *London Stage* project, it was Will Daland who served as the man-machine interface. It might be said that PL/1, the programming language he used, was the interface, but there is no denying it is "artificial," and compared to English, severely limited and specialized. Will was the face that looked both ways: at *The London Stage* and at the IBM 360. He could have learned to be a theatre historian or I could have become a programmer, or, as it actually happened, a running dialog could substitute for either's learning the other's job. Looking back, there are many things I would do differently, mainly in the category of better communication, but I would maintain the division of labor between the scholar and the programmer. Most literary scholars who compute do most of their own programming, I think because it is traditional for humanists to work alone, as opposed to scientists, who like to work in teams. But I wonder if the old lawyers' saying, "He who defends himself in court has a fool for a lawyer," does not apply here. Will had concentrated a whole undergraduate career on computer science. He had done a good deal of programming for pay. He knew how to get the best out of the machines. Since neither of us could easily substitute for the other, a dialog was the best answer. In the course of the dialog I learned a good bit about the machine, and Will learned a good bit about *The London Stage*—and what we learned was only what we had to know. The great universe of what there was to know we could efficiently ignore.

I heartily recommend this kind of man-machine interface. When programmers are set adrift, things tend to go wrong. Explaining a universally acknowledged and widespread disappointment of businessmen in the promise held out by computing, *Communications of The Association For Computing Machinery*, the oracle of the profession, said in 1971, "Technologists [programmers] are least able to manage technology, let alone determine how it should be used. They tend to design extremely sophisticated systems to the limits of technology, rather than simple systems that serve managers well." To prevent disaster "constant top management involvement" is required. One of the chief problems, they continue, is lack of communication between the executive and technical wings of the organization attempting to use the computer.

Can computers think? This is a question that often divides those who compute from those who use computers. I would say, in the first place, that no computer that I have used thinks, and that if someone has a computer that he claims can think, I would agree, not if it could play chess, but if it could write something as good as *King Lear*, or even half as good. Possibly, in the future, mega-minded machines may be built that can do such work, but I doubt it.

There are some computer professionals who would react to this statement as if I had expressed blatant racial prejudice and expressed contempt for man-machine integration ("man-machine symbiosis" is the term they prefer). A year ago, at a computer seminar I attended, the keynote speaker urged that all computers should be tied together. By virtue of the resulting network every user would have at his fingertips the aggregate computing power of the whole system. His cathode ray tube terminal would provide him with cradle to grave education; he could turn to it for news; it would provide him with periodical literature; it would be his personal calculating machine; he would have command of all knowledge—the Library of Congress, the Bureau of Census; lastly it would provide entertainment, play games, display cartoons, create works of art for his delighted eyes. Being a proper government agency, the National Science Foundation also provided someone to speak for the other side of the question. It is still hard for me to believe what the other side of the question was. The speaker was not concerned with the inadequacy of the cathode ray tube as the disseminator of all things needful to man, but with the insurmountable difficulties that stood in the way of this dream. There was never any discussion of why such a network should be established, only how it should be established. The Lawrence faculty would have sent the whole thing back to committee in five minutes. I felt as if I were in another planet.

It is science-fiction characters like this man who blind us to the real need for computing in these times that try men's souls. There are two answers to the problem of increasing population and increasing scarcity. One is regimentation as practiced in totalitarian countries that have chosen to solve the increasing problem of individual differences by making them illegal. The other answer is for governments to increase their capacity to collect, cope with, and adjust to individual differences—in cybernetic terms, to handle feedback. If they cannot do this, they must treat people more and more as if they belonged to an everdiminishing number of classes or general types, until individual differences are no longer collected and recognized in the application of policy, and structure is imposed rather than derived.

In *The Human Use of Human Beings*, Wiener points out that flexible structures survive, rigid ones die. To many people the computer has become a symbol of all that is impersonal, mechanistic, and dehumanizing in our society. Demonstrators pin IBM cards to their shirts. But their real target should be the unimaginative computer system designer. Contrary to the popular myth which holds that computers force us into rigid molds, if used constructively they actually allow for greater individualization of service, simply because of their tremendous capacity to do infinitesimally detailed clerical work in finding, revising, and filing immense numbers of records with the speed of light. It may be that without computerization our institutions cannot survive the onslaught of facts that modern civilization produces and demands attention to.

For instance, in the manufacture and distribution of goods, in the rationing of scarce items, in the conduct of financial affairs, in military service, communications, civic administration, and education, standardization will have to increase with numbers unless means of coping with numbers are developed and flexibility is preserved. Large universities even now may find it easier to meet the needs of students as individuals by using computers to analyze student records and make suggestions rather than relying on the overworked and distracted faculty adviser, who, for want of time to look up the facts, gives all students the same advice. Mass production gave us the single model T Ford. Modern information-handling systems make it possible to offer perhaps as many as several thousand different kinds of Fords, when you consider all the different breeds and the scores of options for each. Just as the telephone, automobile, and airplane extend the human being's spatial scope, the computer extends his memory. Books enable us to extend our knowledge far beyond what can be derived from experience. Computers, if properly applied, further multiply the amount a person can know in the brief span of life allotted to him. As the world increases in numbers and complexity, our need to know becomes greater and so does the difficulty of finding out. The computer is the machine of the hour. But like any invention that radically alters the conditions of existence, its potential for ill is as great as its potential for good. We must cultivate peaceful uses of computers.

The reader may still be wondering how the seminar turned out at the Modern Language Association meeting in Chicago, at which Muriel and Leonard reported on the *London Stage* Information Bank as an aid to research in theatre history, and what impact those hard-won printouts had on those assembled. Well, although Muriel brought her printout to the meeting, she did not treat it specifically, and Leonard, not having time to study his, left it at home and gave a theoretical discussion of the subject. Two months later I heard from a scholar who'd been there that he'd gotten the distinct impression that the project had fallen short of its goals.

I had neglected to transmit through the interface between the *London Stage* Information Bank and its first two users my notion of the importance of Lewis Sawin's message to me an age ago: "Get results."

BCC QA 76 .S3588

Schneider, Ben Ross, 1920-

Travels in computerland